SCHOLASTIC

25 Complex Text Passages to Meet the Common Core

Literature and Informational Texts

Grades 7–8

by Martin Lee and Marcia Miller

NEW YORK ● TORONTO ● LONDON ● AUCKLAND ● SYDNEY
MEXICO CITY ● NEW DELHI ● HONG KONG ● BUENOS AIRES

Teaching Resources

Editor: Mela Ottaiano
Cover design: Scott Davis
Interior design: Kathy Massaro

Interior illustrations: Teresa Anderko (pages 28 and 38). Illustrations copyright © 2014 by Scholastic Inc.

Image credits: page 30 © Videowok_art/iStockphoto; page 34 © PEDRE/istockphoto; page 40 © Margo Harrison/Shutterstock, Inc.; page 50 (top) © Fedor Selivanov/Shutterstock, Inc., (bottom) © Goodluz/Shutterstock, Inc.; page 54 © jeff gynane/Shutterstock, Inc.; page 58 © vgstudio/Shutterstock, Inc.; page 60 © Dirk Ercken/Shutterstock, Inc.; page 64 © sauletas/Shutterstock, Inc.; page 68 © MAC1/Shutterstock, Inc.; page 70 © Andy King/AP Images; page 72 © archana bhartia/Shutterstock, Inc.

Contents

❝ To build a foundation for college and career readiness, students must read widely and deeply from among a broad range of high-quality, increasingly challenging literary and informational texts. Through extensive reading of stories, dramas, poems, and myths from diverse cultures and different time periods, students gain literary and cultural knowledge as well as familiarity with various text structures and elements. By reading texts in history/social studies, science, and other disciplines, students build a foundation of knowledge in these fields that will also give them the background to be better readers in all content areas. Students can only gain this foundation when the curriculum is intentionally and coherently structured to develop rich content knowledge within and across grades. Students also acquire the habits of reading independently and closely, which are essential to their future success. ❞

—COMMON CORE STATE STANDARDS FOR ENGLISH LANGUAGE ARTS, JUNE 2010

25 Complex Text Passages to Meet the Common Core: Literature and Informational Texts—Grades 7–8 includes complex reading passages with companion comprehension question pages for teaching the two types of texts—Literature and Informational—covered in the Common Core State Standards (CCSS) for English Language Arts. The passages and lessons in this book address the rigorous expectations put forth by the CCSS "that students read increasingly complex texts through the grades." This book embraces nine of the ten CCSS College and Career Readiness Anchor Standards for Reading that inform solid instruction for literary and informational texts.

Anchor Standards for Reading

Key Ideas and Details

1 Read closely to determine what the text says explicitly and make logical inferences from it; cite specific textual evidence when writing or speaking to support conclusions drawn from the text.

2 Determine central ideas or themes of a text; summarize key supporting details and ideas.

3 Analyze how and why individuals, events, and ideas develop and interact throughout a text.

Craft and Structure

4 Interpret words and phrases as they are used in a text, including determining technical, connotative, and figurative meanings, and analyze how specific word choices shape meaning or tone.

5 Analyze the structure of texts, including how specific sentences, paragraphs, and larger portions of text relate to each other and the whole.

6 Assess how point of view or purpose shapes the content and style of a text.

Integration of Knowledge and Ideas

7 Integrate and evaluate content presented in diverse media and formats, including visually and quantitatively, as well as in words.

8 Delineate and evaluate the argument and specific claims in a text, including the validity of the reasoning as well as the relevance and sufficiency of the evidence.

Range of Reading and Level of Text Complexity

10 Read and comprehend complex literary and informational texts independently and proficiently.

The materials in this book also address the Language Standards, including skills in the conventions of standard English, knowledge of language, and vocabulary acquisition and use. In addition, students meet Writing Standards as they answer questions about the passages, demonstrating their ability to convey ideas coherently, clearly, and with support from the text. On page 12, you'll find a correlation chart that details how the 25 passages meet specific standards. This information can also be found with the teaching notes for each passage on pages 13–25.

About Text Complexity

The CCSS recommend that students tackle increasingly complex texts to develop and hone their skills and knowledge. Many factors contribute to the complexity of any text.

Text complexity is more intricate than a readability score alone reveals. Most formulas examine sentence length and structure and the number of difficult words. Each formula gives different weight to different factors. Other aspects of text complexity include coherence, organization, motivation, and any prior knowledge readers may bring.

A complex text can be relatively easy to decode, but if it examines complex issues or uses figurative language, the overall text complexity rises. By contrast, a text that uses unfamiliar words may be less daunting if readers can apply word-study skills and context clues effectively to determine meaning.

This triangular model used by the CCSS shows three distinct yet interrelated factors that contribute to text complexity.

CCSS Model of Text Complexity

Qualitative measures consider the complexity of meaning or purpose, structure, language conventionality, and overall clarity.

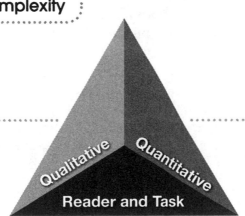

Quantitative measures complexity in terms of word length and frequency, sentence length, and text cohesion. Lexile® algorithms rank this type of complexity on a numerical scale.

Reader and Task considerations refer to such variables as a student's motivation, knowledge, and experience brought to the text, and the purpose, complexity, and types of questions posed.

About the Passages

The 25 reproducible, one-page passages included in this book are divided into two categories. The first 8 passages represent literature (fiction) and are followed by 17 informational texts (nonfiction). Each grouping presents a variety of genres and forms, organizational structures, purposes, tones, and tasks. Consult the table of contents (page 3) to see the scope of genres, forms, and types of content-area texts. The passages within each category are arranged in order of Lexile score (the quantitative measure), from lowest to highest, and fall within the Lexile score ranges recommended for seventh and eighth graders. The Lexile scores for grades 7–8, revised to reflect the more rigorous demands of the CCSS, range from 970 to 1185. For more about determinations of complexity levels, see page 5 and pages 8–9.

Each passage appears on its own page beginning with the title, the genre or form of the passage, and an opening question to give students a focus to keep in mind as they read. Some passages also include visual elements, such as photographs, drawings, illustrations, or tables, as well as typical text elements, such as italics, boldface type, bulleted or numbered lists, subheadings, or sidebars.

The line numbers that appear to the left of each passage will help you and your students readily locate a specific line of text. For example, students might say, "I'm not sure how to pronounce the name here in line 30." They might also include line numbers to identify text evidence when they answer questions about the piece. For example: "The author says in lines 11–13 that…"

The passages are stand-alone texts, and can be used in any order you choose. Feel free to assign passages to individuals, small groups, or the entire class, as best suits your teaching style. However, it's a good idea to preview each passage before you assign it, to ensure that your students have the skills needed to complete it successfully. (See page 10 for a close-reading routine to model for students.)

About the After-Reading Question Pages

The Common Core standards suggest that assessment should involve "text-dependent questions." Questions constructed to meet this demand guide students to cite evidence from the text. They fall into three broad categories: 1) Key Ideas and Details, 2) Craft and Structure, and 3) Integration of Knowledge and Ideas. According to the standards, responses should include claims supported by the text, connections to informational or literary elements found within the text explicitly or by logical implication, and age-appropriate analyses of themes or topics.

Following each passage is a reproducible page with six text-dependent comprehension questions for students to answer after reading. One is a multiple-choice question that calls for a single response and a brief text-based explanation to justify that choice. The other questions are open response items. These address a range of comprehension strategies and skills. Students can revisit the passage to find the evidence they need to answer each question. All questions share the goal of ensuring that students engage in close reading of the text, grasp its key ideas, and provide text-based evidence in their answers. In addition, the questions are formatted to reflect the types of questions that will be asked on standardized tests. The questions generally proceed from easier to more complex:

❋ The **least challenging** questions call for basic understanding and recall of details. They involve referencing the text verbatim or paraphrasing it. This kind of question might also ask students to identify a supporting detail an author did or did not include when making a persuasive argument.

❋ The **mid-level** questions call upon students to use mental processes beyond basic recall. To answer these questions, students may need to use context clues to unlock the meaning of unfamiliar words and phrases (including figurative language), classify or compare information, make inferences, distinguish facts from opinions, or make predictions. Such a question might also ask students to summarize the main idea(s) of a passage.

❋ The **deeper** questions focus on understanding that goes beyond the text. Students may need to recognize the author's tone and purpose, make inferences about the entire passage, or use logic to make predictions. This kind of question might even call upon students to determine why an author began or ended the passage as he or she did.

You may find it useful to have students reference line numbers from the passage for efficiency and clarity when they formulate answers. They can also refer to the line numbers during class discussions. Provide additional paper so students have ample space to write complete and thorough answers.

An answer key (pages 76–80) includes sample answers based on textual evidence and specific line numbers from the passage that support the answers. You might want to review answers with the whole class. This approach provides opportunities for discussion, comparison, extension, reinforcement, and correlation to other skills and lessons in your current plans. Your observations can direct the kinds of review and reinforcement you may want to add to subsequent lessons.

About the Teaching Notes

Each passage in this book is supported by a set of teaching notes found on pages 13–25.

In the left column, you will see the following features for each set of teaching notes.

❋ Grouping (**Literature** or **Informational Text**) and the genre or form of the piece.

❋ **Focus** statement describing the essential purpose of the passage, its main features, areas of emphasis, and what students will gain by reading it.

❋ **Teaching Tips** to help you motivate, support, and guide students before, during, and after reading. These easy-to-use suggestions are by no means exhaustive, and you may choose to add or substitute your own ideas or strategies.

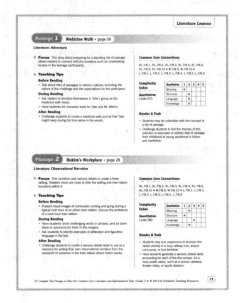

- **Before Reading** tips include ways to introduce a passage, explain a genre, present a topic, discuss a format, introduce key vocabulary, or put a theme in context. A tip may suggest how to engage prior knowledge, connect with similar materials in other curriculum areas, or build motivation.

- **During Reading** tips offer possible procedures to help students work through the text, ideas for highlighting key words or concepts, suggestions for graphic organizers, and so on.

- **After Reading** tips provide follow-up questions, discussion topics, extension activities, further readings, or writing assignments linked to the text.

In the right column, are the essential CCSS connections for the passage sorted according to the specific sections of the document: **RL** (Reading Standards for Literature) or **RI** (Reading Standards for Informational Text), **W** (Writing Standards), and **L** (Language Standards). The CCSS chart on page 12 provides the correlations for the entire book at a glance and a URL for the CCSS website where you can find the specific wording of each skill.

Under the essential CCSS connections, you will find a **Complexity Index**, which offers analytical information about the passage based on the three aspects of text complexity, briefly summarized on the next page.

❊ **Quantitative** value, represented by a Lexile score.

❊ **Qualitative** rating, which appears in a matrix that presents four aspects of this measure:

- **Meaning** for literary texts (single level of meaning ↔ multiple levels of meaning) or **Purpose** for informational texts (explicitly stated purpose ↔ implicit purpose)

- **Structure** (simple ↔ complex organization; simple ↔ complex graphics)

- **Language** (literal ↔ figurative; clear ↔ ambiguous; familiar ↔ unusual; conversational ↔ formal)

- **Knowledge** (life experience; content expectations; cultural or literary background needed)

Each of the above aspects are ranked from 1 to 5, briefly summarized, as follows:

1	2	3	4	5
Simple, clear text; accessible language, ideas, and/or structure	Mostly linear with explicit meaning/purpose; clear structure; moderate vocabulary; assumes some knowledge	May have more than one meaning/purpose; some figurative language; more demanding structure, syntax, language, and/or vocabulary; assumes some knowledge	Multiple meanings/purposes possible; more sophisticated syntax, structure, language, and/or vocabulary; assumes much knowledge	May require inference and/or synthesis; complex structure, syntax, language, and/or vocabulary; assumes extensive knowledge

❊ **Reader and Task** considerations comprise two or more bulleted points. Ideas relating to the reader appear first, followed by specific suggestions for a text-based task. Reader and Task considerations also appear embedded within the teaching notes as well as in the guiding question that opens each passage and in the comprehension questions. Keep in mind that Reader and Task considerations are the most variable of the three measures of text complexity. Reader issues relate to such broad concerns as prior knowledge and experience, cognitive abilities, reading skills, motivation by and engagement with the text, and content and/or theme concerns. Tasks are typically questions to answer, ideas to discuss, or activities to help students navigate and analyze the text, understand key ideas, and deepen comprehension. The same task may be stimulating for some students but daunting to others. Because you know your students best, use your judgment to adjust and revise tasks as appropriate.

Teaching Routine to Support Close Reading

Complex texts become more accessible to readers who are able to use various strategies during the reading process. One of the best ways to scaffold students through this process is to model a close-reading routine.

* **Preview the text.** Help students learn to identify clues about the meaning, purpose, or goal of the text. They can first read the title and the guiding question that precedes the passage. In literary texts, students can scan for characters' names and clues about setting and time frame. In informational texts, students can use features such as paragraph subheadings and supporting photos, illustrations, or other graphics to get a sense of the organization and purpose.

* **Quick-read to get the gist.** Have students do a "run-through" individual reading of the passage to get a sense of it. The quick-read technique can also help students identify areas of confusion or problem vocabulary. You can liken this step to scanning a new store to get a sense of how it is set up, what products it sells, and how you can find what you need.

* **Read closely.** Next, have students read the same piece again, this time with an eye to unlocking its deeper meaning or purpose. For most students, this is the time to use sticky notes, highlighter pens, margin notes, or graphic organizers to help them work their way through the important parts of the text. You might provide text-related graphic organizers, such as T-charts, compare/contrast and Venn diagrams, character and concept maps, cause-and-effect charts, or evidence/conclusion tables.

* **Respond to the text.** Now it's time for students to pull their ideas together and for you to assess their understanding. This may involve summarizing, reading aloud, holding group discussions, debates, or answering written questions. When you assign the after-reading question pages, suggest that students reread questions as needed before they attempt an answer. Encourage them to return to the text as well. Remind students to provide text-based evidence as part of every answer. Finally, consider with students the big ideas of a piece, its message, lesson, or purpose, and think about how to extend learning.

Above all, use the passages and teaching materials in this book to inspire students to become mindful readers—readers who delve deeply into a text to get the most out of it. Help your students recognize that reading is much more than just decoding all the words. Guide them to dig in, think about ideas, determine meaning, and grasp messages.

The following page presents three copies of a reproducible, six-step guide to mindful reading. It is intended as a reusable prompt. Students can keep it at hand to help them recall, apply, and internalize close-reading strategies whenever they read.

25 Complex Text Passages to Meet the Common Core: Literature and Informational Texts, Grades 7–8 © 2014 by Scholastic Teaching Resources

How to Be
A Mindful Reader

Preview the text.
- Set a purpose for reading.

Read carefully.
- Slow down and stay focused.
- Monitor your understanding.

Read again.
- You might notice new information.

Take notes.
- Mark difficult words or phrases.
- Write questions in the margin.
- Make connections between ideas.

Summarize.
- Add headings.
- Jot down the main ideas.
- List the events in sequence.

Think about it.
- Read between the lines. What's the message?
- Do you agree or disagree?
- Has anything been left out?

How to Be
A Mindful Reader

Preview the text.
- Set a purpose for reading.

Read carefully.
- Slow down and stay focused.
- Monitor your understanding.

Read again.
- You might notice new information.

Take notes.
- Mark difficult words or phrases.
- Write questions in the margin.
- Make connections between ideas.

Summarize.
- Add headings.
- Jot down the main ideas.
- List the events in sequence.

Think about it.
- Read between the lines. What's the message?
- Do you agree or disagree?
- Has anything been left out?

How to Be
A Mindful Reader

Preview the text.
- Set a purpose for reading.

Read carefully.
- Slow down and stay focused.
- Monitor your understanding.

Read again.
- You might notice new information.

Take notes.
- Mark difficult words or phrases.
- Write questions in the margin.
- Make connections between ideas.

Summarize.
- Add headings.
- Jot down the main ideas.
- List the events in sequence.

Think about it.
- Read between the lines. What's the message?
- Do you agree or disagree?
- Has anything been left out?

Connections to the Common Core State Standards

As shown in the chart below, the teaching resources in this book will help you meet many of the reading, writing, and language standards for grades 7–8 outlined in the CCSS. For details on these standards, visit the CCSS website: www.corestandards.org/the-standards/.

Passage	RL.7/8.1	RL.7/8.2	RL.7/8.3	RL.7/8.4	RL.7/8.6	RL.7/8.9	RL.7/8.10	RI.7/8.1	RI.7/8.2	RI.7/8.3	RI.7/8.4	RI.7/8.5	RI.7/8.6	RI.7/8.8	RI.7/8.10	W.7/8.9	W.7/8.10	L.7/8.1	L.7/8.2	L.7/8.3	L.7/8.4	L.7/8.5	L.7/8.6
Reading: Literature								**Reading: Informational Text**								**Writing**		**Language**					
1	●	●	●	●	●	●	●									●	●	●	●	●	●	●	●
2	●	●	●	●	●		●									●	●	●	●	●	●	●	●
3	●	●	●	●	●		●									●	●	●	●	●	●	●	●
4	●	●	●	●	●	●	●									●	●	●	●	●	●	●	●
5	●	●	●	●	●		●									●	●	●	●	●	●	●	●
6	●	●	●	●	●		●									●	●	●	●	●	●	●	●
7	●	●	●	●	●		●									●	●	●	●	●	●	●	●
8	●	●	●	●	●	●	●									●	●	●	●	●	●	●	●
9								●	●	●	●	●	●		●	●	●	●	●	●	●	●	●
10								●	●	●	●	●	●	●	●	●	●	●	●	●	●	●	●
11								●	●	●	●	●	●	●	●	●	●	●	●	●	●	●	●
12								●	●	●	●	●	●	●	●	●	●	●	●	●	●	●	●
13								●	●	●	●	●	●		●	●	●	●	●	●	●	●	●
14								●	●	●	●	●	●	●	●	●	●	●	●	●	●	●	●
15								●	●	●	●	●	●	●	●	●	●	●	●	●	●	●	●
16								●	●	●	●	●	●	●	●	●	●	●	●	●	●	●	●
17								●	●	●	●	●	●	●	●	●	●	●	●	●	●	●	●
18								●	●	●	●	●	●	●	●	●	●	●	●	●	●	●	●
19								●	●	●	●	●	●	●	●	●	●	●	●	●	●	●	●
20								●	●	●	●	●	●	●	●	●	●	●	●	●	●	●	●
21								●	●	●	●	●	●	●	●	●	●	●	●	●	●	●	●
22								●	●	●	●	●	●	●	●	●	●	●	●	●	●	●	●
23								●	●	●	●	●	●	●	●	●	●	●	●	●	●	●	●
24								●	●	●	●	●	●	●	●	●	●	●	●	●	●	●	●
25								●	●	●	●	●	●	●	●	●	●	●	●	●	●	●	●

Passage 1 — Medicine Walk • page 26

Literature: Adventure

▶ **Focus** This story about preparing for a daunting rite of passage allows readers to connect with the emotions such an undertaking evokes in the teenage participants.

▶ **Teaching Tips**

Before Reading
- Talk about rites of passages in various cultures, including the nature of the challenge and the expectations for the participant.

During Reading
- Ask readers to envision themselves in Tyler's group as the medicine walk nears.
- Have students list character traits for Tyler and Mr. Melvin.

After Reading
- Challenge students to create a medicine walk journal that Tyler might keep during his time alone in the woods.

Common Core Connections

RL.7/8.1, RL.7/8.2, RL.7/8.3, RL.7/8.4, RL.7/8.6, RL.7/8.9, RL.7/8.10 • W.7/8.9, W.7/8.10 • L.7/8.1, L.7/8.2, L.7/8.3, L.7/8.4, L.7/8.5, L.7/8.6

Complexity Index

Quantitative: Lexile 970

Qualitative	1	2	3	4	5
Meaning	✳				
Structure		✳			
Language		✳			
Knowledge		✳			

Reader & Task

- Students may be unfamiliar with the concept of a rite of passage.
- Challenge students to link the themes of this selection to examples of solitary rites of passage from childhood to young adulthood in fiction and nonfiction.

Passage 2 — Hakim's Workplace • page 28

Literature: Observational Narrative

▶ **Focus** This narrative uses sensory details to create a lively setting. Readers must use clues to infer the setting and how Hakim functions within it.

▶ **Teaching Tips**

Before Reading
- Present visual images of commuters coming and going during a typical rush hour at an urban train station. Discuss the ambience of a rush-hour train station.

During Reading
- Have students circle challenging words or phrases, and jot down ideas or synonyms for them in the margins.
- Ask students to identify examples of alliteration and figurative language in the text.

After Reading
- Challenge students to create a sensory details table to use as a resource for writing their own observational narrative from the viewpoint of someone in the train station where Hakim works.

Common Core Connections

RL.7/8.1, RL.7/8.2, RL.7/8.3, RL.7/8.4, RL.7/8.6, RL.7/8.10 • W.7/8.9, W.7/8.10 • L.7/8.1, L.7/8.2, L.7/8.3, L.7/8.4, L.7/8.5, L.7/8.6

Complexity Index

Quantitative: Lexile 980

Qualitative	1	2	3	4	5
Meaning		✳			
Structure	✳				
Language			✳		
Knowledge		✳			

Reader & Task

- Students may lack experience to envision the varied activity in a busy railway hub, airport concourse, or bus terminal.
- Have students generate a sensory details table, accounting for each of the five senses, for a busy public place, such as a school cafeteria, theater lobby, or sports stadium.

Literature: Folktale

▶ **Focus** In this folktale, students interpret the characters' actions to discover the moral lesson.

▶ **Teaching Tips**

Before Reading
- Review and discuss metaphors and allegories before assigning this folktale.

During Reading
- Have readers summarize the traits of the parrot and Shakra, based on actions or words.
- Suggest that students highlight vivid verbs and descriptive adjectives that enliven this folktale.

After Reading
- Discuss how this tale conveys a life lesson succinctly and without being preachy.

Common Core Connections

RL.7/8.1, RL.7/8.2, RL.7/8.3, RL.7/8.4, RL.7/8.6, RL.7/8.10 • W.7/8.9, W.7/8.10 • L.7/8.1, L.7/8.2, L.7/8.3, L.7/8.4, L.7/8.5, L.7/8.6

Complexity Index

Quantitative: Lexile 990

Qualitative	1	2	3	4	5
Meaning		✳			
Structure		✳			
Language			✳		
Knowledge		✳			

Reader & Task

- Students may be unfamiliar with banyan trees, which figure prominently in many Asian cultures and religions.
- Challenge students to read the folktale as an explicit tale and also as a metaphor (or allegory) that teaches a valuable life lesson.

Literature: Legend

▶ **Focus** This legend gives readers a chance to determine the character traits of a gentleman in colonial times, and debate the nature of his grand gesture.

▶ **Teaching Tips**

Before Reading
- Discuss how medical practices in colonial America were vastly different than they are today. Clarify that the tools and practices were primitive and usually caused great pain.

During Reading
- Ask readers to summarize each paragraph to help them follow the story and remember its details.

After Reading
- Challenge students to extend the story to bring in the woman's likely reactions to the situation and to Allen's gesture.

Common Core Connections

RL.7/8.1, RL.7/8.2, RL.7/8.3, RL.7/8.4, RL.7/8.6, RL.7/8.9, RL.7/8.10 • W.7/8.9, W.7/8.10 • L.7/8.1, L.7/8.2, L.7/8.3, L.7/8.4, L.7/8.5, L.7/8.6

Complexity Index

Quantitative: Lexile 1000

Qualitative	1	2	3	4	5
Meaning		✳			
Structure		✳			
Language			✳		
Knowledge		✳			

Reader & Task

- Students may have some difficulty with the formal language used to tell this legend.
- Have students explain what it meant to be a gentleman in Ethan Allen's time, based on the text.

Literature: Realistic Fiction

▶ **Focus** This piece of realistic fiction offers students the chance to explore how figurative language, precise nouns, and vivid adjective and verbs can create a painterly view of urban life.

▶ **Teaching Tips**

Before Reading
- Discuss the concepts of gentrification and urban renewal, and why people often disagree about the best ways to proceed.

During Reading
- Guide students to appreciate the vivid descriptions, precise nouns, and examples of personification. Suggest that they reread each paragraph to savor sensory details.

After Reading
- Have students write a letter from Jake's point of view trying to persuade his city's mayor to preserve what was left of the waterfront.

Common Core Connections

RL.7/8.1, RL.7/8.2, RL.7/8.3, RL.7/8.4, RL.7/8.6, RL.7/8.10 • W.7/8.9, W.7/8.10 • L.7/8.1, L.7/8.2, L.7/8.3, L.7/8.4, L.7/8.5, L.7/8.6

Complexity Index

Quantitative:
Lexile 1060

Qualitative	1	2	3	4	5
Meaning			✳		
Structure		✳			
Language			✳		
Knowledge			✳		

Reader & Task

- Students may be unfamiliar with the commercial uses of urban waterfronts or with urban renewal projects/gentrification.
- Have students use this selection to debate preserving unique historical structures versus modernizing and updating them for new uses.

Literature: Personal Narrative

▶ **Focus** Readers explore how words have the power to influence a person deeply and unexpectedly in this personal narrative.

▶ **Teaching Tips**

Before Reading
- Share some well-known quotations with students, asking how the words affect them.

During Reading
- Guide students to use context clues and word-analysis strategies to help them determine the meanings of unfamiliar words.

After Reading
- Invite discussion about the narrator, who is unnamed and not clearly described. Suggest that students create a brief character sketch of this person.

Common Core Connections

RL.7/8.1, RL.7/8.2, RL.7/8.3, RL.7/8.4, RL.7/8.6, RL.7/8.10 • W.7/8.9, W.7/8.10 • L.7/8.1, L.7/8.2, L.7/8.3, L.7/8.4, L.7/8.5, L.7/8.6

Complexity Index

Quantitative:
Lexile 1090

Qualitative	1	2	3	4	5
Meaning				✳	
Structure		✳			
Language		✳			
Knowledge		✳			

Reader & Task

- Most students will have some experience with class trips, museum visits, and sightseeing. Some may have been moved by a quotation, song, or work of art.
- Have students write their own personal response to the Malcolm X quotation.

Literature: Nature Anecdote

▶ **Focus** This anecdote, about how insignificant one person can feel in a vast natural wilderness, includes a wealth of geographical and nature terms specific to the American Southwest to help students visualize the setting and connect with the character.

▶ **Teaching Tips**

Before Reading
- Review the third-person point of view. Share other examples of nature writing.

During Reading
- Encourage students to consult a dictionary or online resource to understand the botanical and geographical terminology.

After Reading
- Read aloud the Jack London short story "To Build a Fire." Have students compare and contrast the man in this anecdote with the protagonist in the London story.

Common Core Connections

RL.7/8.1, RL.7/8.2, RL.7/8.3, RL.7/8.4, RL.7/8.6, RL.7/8.10 • W.7/8.9, W.7/8.10 • L.7/8.1, L.7/8.2, L.7/8.3, L.7/8.4, L.7/8.5, L.7/8.6

Complexity Index

Quantitative:
Lexile 1150

Qualitative	1	2	3	4	5
Meaning				✳	
Structure		✳			
Language				✳	
Knowledge				✳	

Reader & Task

- The many descriptive terms and precise nomenclature create a panorama that may be unfamiliar to students.
- Guide students to envision the circumstances in which the man finds himself—the outsider passing through a habitat he can only observe.

Literature: Historical Fiction

▶ **Focus** In this piece of historical fiction, students are introduced to a difficult period in our history by being offered a glimpse into the lives and thoughts of an American family.

▶ **Teaching Tips**

Before Reading
- Tell students to regard this selection as a brief passage from a historical novel.
- Review the Great Depression, President Franklin D. Roosevelt, and the U.S. build up to and participation in World War II.

During Reading
- Guide readers to notice atmospheric details that reveal information about the setting, characters, conflicts, and ways of coping.

After Reading
- Play an audio clip (but no visuals) of a Fireside Chat. Ask students to listen for FDR's candid remarks and reassurances. Challenge them to review the address.

Common Core Connections

RL.7/8.1, RL.7/8.2, RL.7/8.3, RL.7/8.4, RL.7/8.6, RL.7/8.9, RL.7/8.10 • W.7/8.9, W.7/8.10 • L.7/8.1, L.7/8.2, L.7/8.3, L.7/8.4, L.7/8.5, L.7/8.6

Complexity Index

Quantitative:
Lexile 1180

Qualitative	1	2	3	4	5
Meaning			✳		
Structure		✳			
Language				✳	
Knowledge					✳

Reader & Task

- Students who lack familiarity with American history may have difficulty with this selection.
- Have students contemplate the many ways that individuals, families, institutions, and nations respond in the face of difficult news and serious challenges.

Passage 9 — Squishy Foam • page 42

Informational Text: Procedural/Science Recipe

▶ **Focus** An example of easy kitchen chemistry, this recipe utilizes text elements (numbered list, subheadings, boxes, parentheses) to help students follow directions to create a new substance.

▶ **Teaching Tips**

Before Reading
- Discuss chemistry experiments students may have conducted or observed. Review common safety procedures and the importance of following directions accurately.

During Reading
- Read through the materials list together. Clarify the use of parentheses and the style of presenting measurement amounts.
- Have students annotate the steps in any way that would make them easier to follow.

After Reading
- Invite students to make this recipe at home. Discuss how to use proportional reasoning to revise the recipe to yield a smaller amount of squishy foam.

Common Core Connections

RI.7/8.1, RI.7/8.2, RI.7/8.3, RI.7/8.4, RI.7/8.5, RI.7/8.6, RI.7/8.10 • W.7/8.9, W.7/8.10 • L.7/8.1, L.7/8.2, L.7/8.3, L.7/8.4, L.7/8.5, L.7/8.6

Complexity Index

Quantitative: Lexile 990

Qualitative	1	2	3	4	5
Purpose	✳				
Structure			✳		
Language			✳		
Knowledge			✳		

Reader & Task

- Students may be unfamiliar with some materials, vocabulary, or procedures that are part of this project.
- Ask students to think about factors that make instructions easy to understand and follow. Does this recipe meet the criteria?

Passage 10 — Please Re-Boot • page 44

Informational Text: Business Letter

▶ **Focus** This passage exemplifies a well-written letter of complaint, providing students with a model to discuss, analyze, and evaluate.

▶ **Teaching Tips**

Before Reading
- Review the typical elements of a business letter: inside address, date, salutation and closing; pertinent facts, clear and specific request, formal signature.

During Reading
- Ask readers to envision themselves in Raven's boots to grasp the situation.
- Have students indicate strong points, key facts, examples of a productive tone, and unnecessary details, if any.

After Reading
- Challenge students to write a response to Raven from a Customer Service person at Boot Warehouse.
- Have students write a letter of complaint about a product or service they have purchased.

Common Core Connections

RI.7/8.1, RI.7/8.2, RI.7/8.3, RI.7/8.4, RI.7/8.5, RI.7/8.6, RI.7/8.8, RI.7/8.10 • W.7/8.9, W.7/8.10 • L.7/8.1, L.7/8.2, L.7/8.3, L.7/8.4, L.7/8.5, L.7/8.6

Complexity Index

Quantitative: Lexile 1000

Qualitative	1	2	3	4	5
Purpose	✳				
Structure		✳			
Language		✳			
Knowledge			✳		

Reader & Task

- Students may be unfamiliar with the proper form, tone, and style of a business letter.
- Challenge students to evaluate the letter to identify its strengths and strategies.

Informational Text: Cultural Essay

▶ **Focus** This essay, which suggests a potential link between a passion for competition and the American Dream, stimulates thought, discussion, and readers' responses.

▶ **Teaching Tips**

Before Reading
- Have students explain how they would define "The American Dream."

During Reading
- Suggest that readers annotate the essay section by section to indicate questions, highlight points to support or dispute, or identify terminology to investigate.

After Reading
- Have small groups debate the essay. Challenge them to propose a counterargument (whether they support it or not) to the writer's concern about excessive competition.

Common Core Connections

RI.7/8.1, RI.7/8.2, RI.7/8.3, RI.7/8.4, RI.7/8.5, RI.7/8.6, RI.7/8.8, RI.7/8.10 • W.7/8.9, W.7/8.10 • L.7/8.1, L.7/8.2, L.7/8.3, L.7/8.4, L.7/8.5, L.7/8.6

Complexity Index

Quantitative:
Lexile 1020

Qualitative	1	2	3	4	5
Purpose			*		
Structure		*			
Language			*		
Knowledge			*		

Reader & Task

- Students may be unaware that people have pursued competitive activities of many kinds throughout human history.
- Challenge students to formulate a response to the essay in which they address the writer's views, connections, and concerns.

Informational Text: Friendly Letter

▶ **Focus** In this friendly letter, students discover how the informal conversational style of the letter writer reveals much about herself and the recipient.

▶ **Teaching Tips**

Before Reading
- Compare and contrast business letters and friendly letters. Also contrast the features of a hand-written letter with those of e-mail or text messages.

During Reading
- Ask students to identify examples of irony, exaggeration, and wit in the letter. How do these elements help convey the writer's point of view?

After Reading
- Have pairs talk about the kinds of responses Jamie might offer. Then have individuals write response letters from Jamie's viewpoint.

Common Core Connections

RI.7/8.1, RI.7/8.2, RI.7/8.3, RI.7/8.4, RI.7/8.5, RI.7/8.6, RI.7/8.8, RI.7/8.10 • W.7/8.9, W.7/8.10 • L.7/8.1, L.7/8.2, L.7/8.3, L.7/8.4, L.7/8.5, L.7/8.6

Complexity Index

Quantitative:
Lexile 1030

Qualitative	1	2	3	4	5
Purpose		*			
Structure	*				
Language			*		
Knowledge		*			

Reader & Task

- Students may not have much experience writing long friendly letters.
- Have students describe how a writer's voice may change depending on the piece's intended audience. How might Iris's style and tone change if she were writing an article about theater camp?

Informational Text: Historical Essay

▶ **Focus**   Students examine an ever-changing subject from historical, cultural, and sociological perspectives in this essay.

▶ **Teaching Tips**

Before Reading
- Have students preview the text by examining the two photographs and the paragraph subheadings.

During Reading
- Ask readers to jot down questions or margin notes that come to mind as they read.

After Reading
- Discuss the questions students generated and ways to answer them.
- Challenge students to cite examples that show changes in written language even in their own lifetimes (for example, texting, neologisms, abbreviations, slang).

Common Core Connections

RI.7/8.1, RI.7/8.2, RI.7/8.3, RI.7/8.4, RI.7/8.5, RI.7/8.6, RI.7/8.10 • W.7/8.9, W.7/8.10 • L.7/8.1, L.7/8.2, L.7/8.3, L.7/8.4, L.7/8.5, L.7/8.6

Complexity Index

Quantitative: Lexile 1040

Qualitative	1	2	3	4	5
Purpose			✲		
Structure		✲			
Language			✲		
Knowledge				✲	

Reader & Task

- Much of the information in this essay may be new to students.
- Encourage students to synthesize the ideas about ever-evolving language to reflect upon their own experiences with the written word.

Informational Text: Movie Review

▶ **Focus**   This student-written movie review offers readers a chance to review the reviewer, based on the tone, word choice, and conclusions offered.

▶ **Teaching Tips**

Before Reading
- Talk about the typical components of a movie review.

During Reading
- Have students use two different markers to highlight facts in one color, opinions in another.

After Reading
- Invite students who have seen the 2012 film *Lincoln* to compare the review to their own responses to the film. Invite all students to review the review critically.

Common Core Connections

RI.7/8.1, RI.7/8.2, RI.7/8.3, RI.7/8.4, RI.7/8.5, RI.7/8.6, RI.7/8.8, RI.7/8.10 • W.7/8.9, W.7/8.10 • L.7/8.1, L.7/8.2, L.7/8.3, L.7/8.4, L.7/8.5, L.7/8.6

Complexity Index

Quantitative: Lexile 1050

Qualitative	1	2	3	4	5
Purpose		✲			
Structure		✲			
Language			✲		
Knowledge				✲	

Reader & Task

- Readers may be unfamiliar with the politically charged theme of the movie being reviewed, or the dramatic versus historical details the reviewer mentions.
- Have students question whether statements in the review are based on fact or opinion.

Informational Text: Persuasive Essay

▶ **Focus** This passage allows students to examine how the author creates a passionate persuasive essay by using colorful and emotional language, effective idioms, historical detail, comparisons, and rising drama to gain supporters.

▶ **Teaching Tips**

Before Reading
● Clarify the meaning of suffrage (the right to vote).
● Discuss the characteristics of a powerful piece of persuasive writing.

During Reading
● Help readers with idioms they may not know (for example, "It's high time…").
● Have students circle examples of highly charged words and phrases.

After Reading
● Challenge students to write a response to answer: Do you support the idea of a monument to honor the Silent Sentinels? Have them refer to the text to support their position.

Common Core Connections

RI.7/8.1, RI.7/8.2, RI.7/8.3, RI.7/8.4, RI.7/8.5, RI.7/8.6, RI.7/8.8, RI.7/8.10 ● W.7/8.9, W.7/8.10 ● L.7/8.1, L.7/8.2, L.7/8.3, L.7/8.4, L.7/8.5, L.7/8.6

Complexity Index

Quantitative: Lexile 1070

Qualitative	1	2	3	4	5
Purpose		✳			
Structure		✳			
Language				✳	
Knowledge				✳	

Reader & Task

● Because women have had the vote for nearly a century now, students may not appreciate the long and arduous struggle that suffragists endured.
● Have students critically examine the arguments the writer presents. Encourage them to consider which people or causes merit a national monument.

Informational Text: Persuasive Speech

▶ **Focus** Readers will analyze the main idea, structure, and effectiveness of a public speech.

▶ **Teaching Tips**

Before Reading
● Have students picture a public space where a panel of speakers will answer the same question before an audience.

During Reading
● Ask students to find evidence that the text is a speech.
● Ask readers to distinguish facts from opinions. They can mark F or O in the margins.

After Reading
● Divide students into small groups to hold their own discussion of the question. Provide them time to prepare their arguments. Ask them to draw comparisons between their points and those of the author.

Common Core Connections

RI.7/8.1, RI.7/8.2, RI.7/8.3, RI.7/8.4, RI.7/8.5, RI.7/8.6, RI.7/8.8, RI.7/8.10 ● W.7/8.9, W.7/8.10 ● L.7/8.1, L.7/8.2, L.7/8.3, L.7/8.4, L.7/8.5, L.7/8.6

Complexity Index

Quantitative: Lexile 1080

Qualitative	1	2	3	4	5
Purpose				✳	
Structure			✳		
Language				✳	
Knowledge			✳		

Reader & Task

● Students may not be familiar with public panel discussions that examine issues.
● Have students evaluate the speech for its main idea, structure, and use of language.

Informational Text: Advertisement/Nutrition Label

▶ **Focus** This example of an ad for an energy drink challenges readers to think critically about its claims and to evaluate the given data for hidden messages.

▶ **Teaching Tips**

Before Reading
- Discuss the importance of reading product labels and information very carefully, and point out that the goals of advertising may conflict with a customer's needs.

During Reading
- Have students jot down questions or comments that the ad generates.
- Guide students to read the nutrition label and ingredients list carefully and critically.

After Reading
- Invite students to share and discuss the questions they generated for question 6.
- Have students find a print ad. Challenge them to apply the critical reading skills they used in this lesson to evaluate it and share their analysis with the class.

Common Core Connections

RI.7/8.1, RI.7/8.2, RI.7/8.3, RI.7/8.4, RI.7/8.5, RI.7/8.6, RI.7/8.8, RI.7/8.10 • W.7/8.9, W.7/8.10 • L.7/8.1, L.7/8.2, L.7/8.3, L.7/8.4, L.7/8.5, L.7/8.6

Complexity Index

Quantitative: Lexile 1090

Qualitative	1	2	3	4	5
Purpose				✳	
Structure				✳	
Language				✳	
Knowledge				✳	

Reader & Task

- Students, unsophisticated about marketing and advertising, may not realize that the best information about a product appears in its labels, not in its ads.
- Ask students to "read between the lines" to detect the truth about Perk-Up.

Informational Text: Technology Essay

▶ **Focus** Students consider how this challenging essay provides scientific, cultural, and historical data, and raises legitimate concerns about a current topic without taking sides.

▶ **Teaching Tips**

Before Reading
- Engage prior knowledge about the Frankenstein story, including the message of the classic tale and visual representations related to it.

During Reading
- Have students make a Pro-Con chart with details from the text as they read.
- Provide and encourage the use of dictionaries or other reference materials as needed to assist comprehension.

After Reading
- Assign students to research this topic by interviewing workers at local health food stores, markets, produce stands, as well as scientists, farmers, or nutritionists.

Common Core Connections

RI.7/8.1, RI.7/8.2, RI.7/8.3, RI.7/8.4, RI.7/8.5, RI.7/8.6, RI.7/8.8, RI.7/8.10 • W.7/8.9, W.7/8.10 • L.7/8.1, L.7/8.2, L.7/8.3, L.7/8.4, L.7/8.5, L.7/8.6

Complexity Index

Quantitative: Lexile 1100

Qualitative	1	2	3	4	5
Purpose				✳	
Structure				✳	
Language				✳	
Knowledge					✳

Reader & Task

- Students may need support to handle vocabulary, abstract concepts, long and complicated sentences, and the critical thinking required to make sense of this essay.
- Have students summarize both sides of the GMO question, offer their views on the topic, and/or describe additional information they would seek before deciding.

Informational Text: Personal Essay

▶ **Focus** Readers make inferences and draw conclusions about a student by evaluating a personal essay written as a letter of application.

▶ **Teaching Tips**

Before Reading

- Explain that a personal essay is often a required part of the process of admission to certain schools. Discuss the elements of such an essay.

During Reading

- Have students determine why the letter begins with such a vague salutation.
- Ask readers to highlight transitional words/phrases that help make the ideas in the essay flow coherently.

After Reading

- Share the opinions students have formed about Eleni based on the essay. Challenge them to formulate helpful questions an admissions person might ask her.

Common Core Connections

RI.7/8.1, RI.7/8.2, RI.7/8.3, RI.7/8.4, RI.7/8.5, RI.7/8.6, RI.7/8.8, RI.7/8.10 • W.7/8.9, W.7/8.10 • L.7/8.1, L.7/8.2, L.7/8.3, L.7/8.4, L.7/8.5, L.7/8.6

Complexity Index

Quantitative: Lexile 1110

Qualitative	1	2	3	4	5
Purpose			✳		
Structure				✳	
Language			✳		
Knowledge			✳		

Reader & Task

- Some students may be unaware that eighth graders can apply to specific high schools, and that a personal essay is often part of the process.
- Ask students to identify the specific details in Eleni's letter that led them to form an opinion about her.

Informational Text: Art Essay

▶ **Focus** This essay presents ways to compare and contrast two broad categories of art and encourages readers to think differently about art.

▶ **Teaching Tips**

Before Reading

- Display examples of paintings by Pablo Picasso and by Grandma Moses. Allow students to describe, respond to, and voice their preferences about these works.

During Reading

- Have students make margin notes by writing *M* beside words or phrases that motivate, *I* for those that inform, and *P* for those that persuade.
- Encourage students to reread paragraphs to deepen understanding.

After Reading

- Assign students to write response essays with their views on the theme and conclusion presented in this piece.

Common Core Connections

RI.7/8.1, RI.7/8.2, RI.7/8.3, RI.7/8.4, RI.7/8.5, RI.7/8.6, RI.7/8.8, RI.7/8.10 • W.7/8.9, W.7/8.10 • L.7/8.1, L.7/8.2, L.7/8.3, L.7/8.4, L.7/8.5, L.7/8.6

Complexity Index

Quantitative: Lexile 1130

Qualitative	1	2	3	4	5
Purpose				✳	
Structure				✳	
Language				✳	
Knowledge					✳

Reader & Task

- Prior knowledge and experience play a role in students' ability to grasp this piece.
- Encourage students to grasp similarities and differences between fine art and folk art.

Informational Text: Online Editorial

▶ **Focus** This passage, an opinion piece about an issue of public interest, asks readers to evaluate its effectiveness.

▶ **Teaching Tips**

Before Reading

- Review the features and style of effective editorials.
- Explain that some localities permit residents to vote on public expenditures.

During Reading

- Have students reread each paragraph to ensure that they grasp its main idea.
- Ask students to create a graphic organizer that maps the editorial's structure.

After Reading

- Challenge students to write a parallel editorial that favors Proposition 43.

Common Core Connections

RI.7/8.1, RI.7/8.2, RI.7/8.3, RI.7/8.4, RI.7/8.5, RI.7/8.6, RI.7/8.8, RI.7/8.10 • W.7/8.9, W.7/8.10 • L.7/8.1, L.7/8.2, L.7/8.3, L.7/8.4, L.7/8.5, L.7/8.6

Complexity Index

Quantitative: Lexile 1140

Qualitative	1	2	3	4	5
Purpose				✳	
Structure			✳		
Language				✳	
Knowledge				✳	

Reader & Task

- This piece presents a type of public issue students may never have considered before.
- Students should identify the parts of a good editorial: state the issue, present both sides, make a well-supported case for one view, end with a forceful call to action.

Informational Text: Biographical Sketch

▶ **Focus** This biographical sketch asks readers to make inferences about the character traits of the different people mentioned in the sketch, based on their actions.

▶ **Teaching Tips**

Before Reading

- Discuss similarities and differences among biographies, personal anecdotes, and biographical sketches.

During Reading

- Ask readers to highlight idioms, expressions, and phrases that relate to flying, challenges, and achievements.
- Invite students to look for answers to the focus question.

After Reading

- Have students imagine being journalists at the airfield on the day of Callum's solo flight. They should formulate questions to ask Callum, his parents, and instructor.

Common Core Connections

RI.7/8.1, RI.7/8.2, RI.7/8.3, RI.7/8.4, RI.7/8.5, RI.7/8.6, RI.7/8.8, RI.7/8.10 • W.7/8.9, W.7/8.10 • L.7/8.1, L.7/8.2, L.7/8.3, L.7/8.4, L.7/8.5, L.7/8.6

Complexity Index

Quantitative: Lexile 1150

Qualitative	1	2	3	4	5
Purpose			✳		
Structure				✳	
Language			✳		
Knowledge				✳	

Reader & Task

- Students may be unfamiliar with the world of aviation, but the notion of a teen setting and achieving a remarkable goal should inspire most readers.
- Challenge students to "read between the lines" to summarize the traits of the subject, Callum Lavender, his parents, and his flight instructor.

Informational Text: Sports History Article

▶ **Focus** This article, which offers a look back at an extraordinary moment in sports history, asks readers to draw inferences, ponder language use, and evaluate its effectiveness.

▶ **Teaching Tips**

Before Reading

- Point out that during the tense Cold War years, the United States and former Soviet Union were deeply mistrustful opponents in a rivalry for military power and influence.

During Reading

- Have readers make a chart contrasting the U.S. and Soviet hockey teams.
- Encourage readers to list questions to ask to clarify aspects of this event.

After Reading

- Challenge students to research contemporary descriptions or analyses of this game.

Common Core Connections

RI.7/8.1, RI.7/8.2, RI.7/8.3, RI.7/8.4, RI.7/8.5, RI.7/8.6, RI.7/8.8, RI.7/8.10 • W.7/8.9, W.7/8.10 • L.7/8.1, L.7/8.2, L.7/8.3, L.7/8.4, L.7/8.5, L.7/8.6

Complexity Index

Quantitative: Lexile 1160

Qualitative	1	2	3	4	5
Purpose			✳		
Structure			✳		
Language			✳		
Knowledge				✳	

Reader & Task

- Students unaware of the strained geopolitical atmosphere in 1980 may not fully appreciate what a symbolic victory this was for the United States.
- Challenge students to view the "miracle on ice" on two levels: literally as an exciting upset sports victory, and figuratively as an international victory.

Informational Text: Magazine Article

▶ **Focus** This inspirational article challenges readers to consider the philosophical, emotional, and sociological possibilities of a groundbreaking music program.

▶ **Teaching Tips**

Before Reading

- If possible, motivate students by showing a brief online video clip about the remarkable El Sistema program.

During Reading

- Tell students to keep the focus question in mind as they read to understand what El Sistema seeks for its participants other than musical achievement. They can make margin notes or highlight supporting details.

After Reading

- Assign students to write a compare/contrast essay that examines constant elements of the program with ones that vary as participants get older.

Common Core Connections

RI.7/8.1, RI.7/8.2, RI.7/8.3, RI.7/8.4, RI.7/8.5, RI.7/8.6, RI.7/8.8, RI.7/8.10 • W.7/8.9, W.7/8.10 • L.7/8.1, L.7/8.2, L.7/8.3, L.7/8.4, L.7/8.5, L.7/8.6

Complexity Index

Quantitative: Lexile 1170

Qualitative	1	2	3	4	5
Purpose				✳	
Structure				✳	
Language					✳
Knowledge					✳

Reader & Task

- Students may be unused to thinking about music beyond its entertainment value.
- Have students discuss how a musical training program like El Sistema could influence a participant's life beyond the musical realm.

Informational Text: Science Essay

▶ **Focus** In telling an unusual true story of a family experiment about time, this essay challenges readers' comprehension skills, scientific understanding, and imagination.

▶ **Teaching Tips**

Before Reading

- Discuss the title to ensure that students understand the meanings of *eccentric* and *staycation*. Include the meaning of *eccentric* as it relates to orbital paths.

During Reading

- Encourage readers to envision themselves taking part in the experiment.
- Remind students that the data table complements the essay by providing supporting information. Have them determine the meaning of *synodic*.

After Reading

- Assign students to research the Mars Rover program, flight director Dr. David Oh, or the scientific uses for the data gathered by Curiosity, and present their findings.

Common Core Connections

RI.7/8.1, RI.7/8.2, RI.7/8.3, RI.7/8.4, RI.7/8.5, RI.7/8.6, RI.7/8.8, RI.7/8.10 • W.7/8.9, W.7/8.10 • L.7/8.1, L.7/8.2, L.7/8.3, L.7/8.4, L.7/8.5, L.7/8.6

Complexity Index

Quantitative:
Lexile 1180

Qualitative	1	2	3	4	5
Purpose				✳	
Structure					✳
Language					✳
Knowledge					✳

Reader & Task

- Many demanding terms, long sentences, and a complex topic will challenge readers.
- Challenge students to analyze the essay for ways that it supports each word in its title.

Name _____ Date _____

Medicine Walk

What is the purpose of a medicine walk?

1　　The daunting task jumbled Tyler's thoughts: *How could I spend 16 hours—*
2　*including overnight—alone in the wooded state park? What if I have no "mature*
3　*problem-solver" inside me? How will I succeed if I'm scared silly or worried whether*
4　*I'll ever find my way back?*
5　　But Tyler had no choice in this matter. Every young man in his family, as far
6　back as anyone could recall, had undertaken his own "medicine walk." Each
7　boy more than survived the challenge; in fact, each recalled the demanding
8　experience with fierce pride and acknowledged how eye-opening it had been.
9　Tyler liked being on his own, but preferred the security of his cell phone or at
10　least a sturdy flashlight to solitary exploration.
11　　Mr. Melvin served as Tyler's coach. He led a reluctant group of 13-year-olds
12　whose families wanted them to experience a medicine walk as an exercise in
13　self-reliance. "I did my own version of this when I was thirteen," he shared. "My
14　folks called it a vision quest, but to me it began as aimless wandering. I was
15　allowed to bring very little with me, but I did carry the voices of the elders in my
16　head as I explored. As my medicine walk day went on, my own voice emerged,
17　and it served me well. My task today is to help you find your own inner strength
18　to accompany you on your journey."
19　　Tyler understood that people learn by experience, but feared that the
20　inexperienced couldn't possibly have the resources to extract themselves from a
21　tangle. The what-ifs tormented him; he fought back tears of shame for feeling
22　so frightened.
23　　Mr. Melvin stayed calm and confident as a model to the boys. He prepared
24　the group by sharing maps of the area, which indicated clear boundaries
25　beyond which walkers could not go, and noted occasional trail markers that
26　would help orient the walkers. The group learned to identify animal tracks,
27　recognize edible plants, and build a quick and simple shelter. Mr. Melvin
28　also helped them discover ways to invite curiosity and wonder instead of fear
29　and doubt. Together they took group practice walks, each one a bit more
30　challenging than the previous one.
31　　On the last meeting before the intimidating medicine walk, the group
32　held a candid question-and-answer session in which each participant was
33　encouraged to express his fears or concerns. Mr. Melvin modeled steady support
34　and patience, saying, "Remember, you're not crossing a storm-tossed ocean
35　on a rickety raft. You'll be in a limited area for a fixed period of time. You will
36　begin as a group at 9:00 Saturday morning. Then you'll separate and explore
37　anywhere inside the designated area. You will spend the night wherever
38　you choose, in a shelter you will make, eating the food you bring with you,
39　and drinking fresh water you collect from the creek. You'll be free with your
40　thoughts and dreams. We'll reunite at 1:00 P.M. Sunday, exactly where we
41　began. Any questions?"

Name _____ Date _____

Medicine Walk

▶ **Answer each question. Give evidence from the adventure.**

1 Why was Tyler on the verge of crying (lines 21–22)?

○ A. He lacked experience being on his own.

○ B. He felt forced into making a medicine walk.

○ C. He was embarrassed that it was his first medicine walk.

○ D. He felt ashamed for feeling so fearful.

What evidence in the text helped you answer? _____

_____

_____

2 What makes Mr. Melvin an ideal coach for Tyler and the group? _____

_____

_____

3 Describe the nature of a medicine walk and its overarching purpose. _____

_____

_____

_____

4 Why is *mature problem-solver* (lines 2 and 3) within quotation marks? _____

_____

_____

5 What word in this passage could be synonymous with *daunting* (line 1)? Explain. _____

_____

_____

6 How would you describe Mr. Melvin's approach to preparing the boys for their medicine walk?

_____

_____

_____

Name _____ Date _____

Hakim's Workplace

In what ways does Hakim broaden his perspective as he works?

1 Hakim spent much of his day looking down, attending to his job. He wore
2 a thick denim apron over a T-shirt and sturdy work pants. His right hand was
3 enclosed in a close-fitting black leather glove. On his left, he sported a lighter
4 glove, which at the moment clasped a spray bottle, a key tool of his trade.
5 Within easy reach rested a weathered wooden box containing brushes, tins of
6 polish, applicators, rags, and shine-cloths.
7   The bustle that went on around Hakim entered his consciousness auditorily.
8 He experienced his surroundings through the announcements of arrivals and
9 departures, the prattling of passersby, the rumblings of rolling suitcases. But
10 when he straightened up and looked about he saw essentially the same thing
11 each day: people walking briskly to the trains or coming, more casually, from
12 them. He glimpsed them hustling along alone, speaking into their cell phones,
13 or carrying coffee in one hand, a briefcase in the other. He noticed pairs chatting
14 enthusiastically, their reunions or impromptu business conferences already
15 underway. He spied bewildered families, unused to chaos, drifting in anxious
16 crowds. Yes, he observed basically the same things, even some of the same
17 people, every day. They all belonged here; it all made sense. When something
18 broke the usual rhythms, even slightly, it engaged him.
19   That's what happened this morning when Hakim stood up and stretched his
20 weary back and stiff shoulders. He spotted two yipping teenage girls in purple
21 jeans racing toward the concourse. A few steps behind them scurried a frazzled
22 woman, struggling to keep her balance in too-high heels. Trailing just behind
23 her a young boy dragged a tortoise-shaped rolling backpack, trying doggedly
24 to keep it upright and keep pace with the woman. *Why all the fuss and bother?*
25 Hakim thought, smiling inwardly. *Are these people together or merely a random*
26 *collection of travelers in a rush?* Hakim didn't bother to answer, but pivoted slowly,
27 bent down, and resumed the task before him: breathing new life into a scuffed
28 and neglected pair of mahogany oxfords.

Name _____ Date _____

Hakim's Workplace

▶ **Answer each question. Give evidence from the narrative.**

1 Which of these words from the narrative is an example of onomatopoeia?

○ A. clasped (line 4)   ○ B. auditorily (line 7)   ○ C. rhythms (line 18)   ○ D. yipping (line 20)

How did you determine your response? _____

_____

_____

2 What is Hakim's job and where does he work? _____

_____

_____

3 In line 17, the author writes, "They all belonged here; it all made sense." How does this sentence capture the setting of the narrative?

_____

_____

_____

4 Hakim experiences his environment *auditorily* (line 7). Explain what this means. _____

_____

_____

5 Describe Hakim's attitude toward his surroundings. _____

_____

_____

_____

6 Suggest a possible explanation to link the yipping teens, the frazzled woman, and the young boy dragging a backpack (lines 20–24).

_____

_____

_____

_____

Name _____ Date _____

The Steadfast Parrot
Buddhist Folktale

How does the title accurately represent the theme of this tale?

1   A petite parrot lived contentedly in a colossal banyan
2   tree that supplied her every physical comfort she required.
3   Its emerald leaves veiled her from the blazing sun. Its
4   undulating branches made gentle creaking rhythms that
5   soothed her concerns. Its cool bark refreshed her weary claws,
6   and its moist and plentiful fruit satisfied her hunger.
7   The parrot appreciated the bounties her beloved banyan
8   provided. Every night before she tucked her head beneath her
9   feathered wing, she expressed gratitude. "Beloved banyan, I
10   honor you for welcoming me into your comforting fullness.
11   My life with you is serene, contented, and free with your
12   gracious hospitality. Never shall I abandon you for another."
13   Then the parrot would close her eyes and drift to sleep as the
14   evening winds rustled the tree's leaves.
15   Shakra, King of the gods, overheard the parrot's thankful words each evening,
16   but wondered whether she truly meant everything she said. So he decided to test
17   her loyalty. During the night, Shakra caused the enormous banyan to wither,
18   turning its once-green leaves brown and brittle. Dust coated the branches where
19   life-giving morning dew once collected.
20   As stunned as the parrot was by this abrupt and shocking change, she kept
21   her composure. Perched among its dead leaves, she vowed not to abandon the
22   lifeless tree. Recalling better days, she flitted from branch to branch, flooded
23   with fond memories. Despite the banyan's desolate appearance, the parrot could
24   envision it only as it had been—lush, verdant, cool, protective.
25   The determined creature resolved to remain. As days passed, the brutal sun
26   bore down on the parrot but could not scorch her calm. Though she yearned
27   for the dense leaves and refreshing shade, she pledged: "Friends don't abandon
28   friends when ill fortune strikes. Over time, fortunes may change, but I shall
29   remain faithful."
30   When Shakra observed the parrot's perseverance, he became certain that
31   the bird had spoken truthfully. He summoned a golden breeze to envelop the
32   banyan. At once newborn buds emerged, fresh leaves unfurled, fruits sprouted
33   and ripened, and ashen dust wafted away.
34   The astonished parrot released a blissful squawk to find herself sheltered
35   again by the banyan she recognized. "Parrot," said Shakra, "you have proven
36   your loyalty and devotion. Your steadfast commitment permitted this tree to
37   revive. You are small, but within you beats a true heart."
38   Shakra disappeared behind a cloud. The grateful parrot bowed her head,
39   sipped fresh dew, rubbed her beak along the cool bark, and listened to the
40   whispering leaves. "Oh banyan, my love was true and deep," she crooned.
41   "My banyan, my promise I did steadfastly keep."

Name _____ Date _____

The Steadfast Parrot

▶ **Answer each question. Give evidence from the folktale.**

1 After Shakra changed the banyan, the parrot "kept her composure" (lines 20 and 21). Which of the following is an example of keeping one's composure?

    ○ A. maintaining one's balance on a narrow beam   ○ C. exploding in anger

    ○ B. staying calm in an emergency   ○ D. writing music for wind instruments

What evidence in the text helped you answer? _____

_____

2 The banyan had *undulating* branches (line 4). Use the photo to help give the meaning of *undulate*. Then describe something else in nature that undulates.

_____

_____

_____

3 What does Shakra's test of the parrot reveal about him? _____

_____

_____

4 Give two examples of personification in this folktale. _____

_____

_____

5 Compare the relationship between the parrot and the banyan with the relationship between close friends.

_____

_____

_____

6 The folktale uses the metaphor of the steadfast parrot to convey a lesson. What is the lesson?

_____

_____

_____

Name _____ Date _____

Ethan Allen, Gentleman

Legend From Vermont

What traits characterize a "gentleman" in this legend?

1   You may be familiar with Ethan Allen as the commander of the
2   Vermont Green Mountain Boys. He led them to defeat the British at Fort
3   Ticonderoga in 1775, early in the American Revolutionary War. Indeed,
4   he was a heroic patriot, an astute businessman, and a savvy politician.
5   Some recall that he had a gruff manner and spent too much time in local
6   taverns. But a little-known fact about Allen is that he could be quite the
7   gentleman. You never knew whether or where he might reveal his gallant
8   side, or who or what might prompt him to do so.
9   Allen once visited a friend in Bennington, where that man served as the
10 town's dentist. As the companions shared stories, a woman in great distress
11 appeared at the dentist's door. She complained of a terrible toothache that
12 was getting worse by the hour. Allen stepped aside as the dentist escorted
13 the woman to his examining chair. She hesitantly sat as the dentist
14 checked the throbbing tooth. It was quite apparent that the tooth would
15 have to be pulled to relieve the woman's agony.
16 Though the woman was acquainted with the dentist's fine reputation,
17 the very sight of the terrifying tools he was preparing alarmed her. She
18 began to fidget in the chair, and finally held up her hands to restrain the
19 dentist, who tilted his head to one side to consider other options. Alas, he
20 could think of none.
21 At that moment, Ethan Allen approached the frightened woman,
22 offering a deep and courteous bow. "Madame," he said confidently, "I can
23 vouch for my friend, an experienced dentist whose skills will soon release
24 you from your suffering. I beseech you to reconsider." But the woman,
25 already near panic, refused to permit the dentist to continue.
26 "My good woman," Allen coaxed gently, "allow me to prove that you
27 have absolutely nothing to fear." With this, Allen helped the woman rise
28 from the dentist's chair and reclined in it himself. As she regained her
29 composure, Allen instructed his friend to remove a tooth, any tooth, to
30 demonstrate the folly of her concern.
31 So the dentist did precisely that—he quickly and without a sound
32 extracted one of Ethan Allen's perfectly healthy teeth as the woman
33 observed. When the dentist completed the task, Allen rose, bowed to the
34 woman and proclaimed, "There! You see, I didn't feel it at all." Allen
35 smiled, stepped aside, and gestured toward the chair.
36 Now reassured, the woman reclaimed the chair and permitted the
37 dentist to extract her aching tooth. Ethan Allen stood resolutely by her side
38 to offer comfort and support as he suffered in utter silence.

Name _____ Date _____

Ethan Allen, Gentleman

▶ **Answer each question. Give evidence from the legend.**

1 Which pair of words from the legend are most nearly synonyms?

○ A. *gruff* (line 5) and *courteous* (line 22)   ○ C. *vouch* (line 23) and *beseech* (line 24)

○ B. *astute* (line 4) and *savvy* (line 4)   ○ D. *hesitantly* (line 13) and *resolutely* (line 37)

How did you determine your response? _____

_____

_____

2 What made the once-fearful woman willing to return to the dentist's chair? _____

_____

_____

3 This legend is over 200 years old. How does the tone and word choice used in its telling help make it sound authentic?

_____

_____

_____

4 Why did the experienced dentist have no others options to help the woman? _____

_____

_____

5 In your opinion, did Ethan Allen behave gallantly or deceitfully? Explain. _____

_____

_____

_____

6 Based on this legend, how would you describe a gentleman? _____

_____

_____

Name _____ Date _____

Jake's Piers

Why is Jake so drawn to the piers?

1 When Jake was 14 his family moved from the suburbs into the big city. His
2 new home was located along the river in what had once been an industrial
3 area filled with factories and warehouses near old rail lines and shipping
4 piers. His new neighborhood was in the process of gentrifying. Its massive
5 industrial buildings were now being converted into modern apartments. Tiny
6 boutiques and chic eateries were trickling in, welcoming adventurous clientele
7 from all over to the quaint cobblestone streets of this once bleak landscape.

8 Jake's own apartment was a loft-like space in a recently defrosted
9 refrigeration warehouse. Since the renovations were incomplete, Jake liked to
10 sneak off with his flashlight to explore unoccupied residences. But what he
11 liked best was to cross the street to the piers.

12 Jake could see these dilapidated structures from his window, remnants of
13 another time. Once there to greet the freighters and barges, they were now
14 rotting away, home to weeds, broken glass, vermin, and garbage. They stood
15 there, sad and silent, on barnacle-covered pilings. The chain-link fences that
16 guarded them were no match for a curious teenager.

17 On the piers Jake could be alone with his thoughts in the eerie silence. The
18 city was but a few hundred yards behind him, but its bustle and clamor were
19 inaudible. All Jake could hear as he sat at the far edge with his feet hanging
20 over the water was the rhythmic slapping of the tide, the squawk of the sea
21 birds who kept him company, and the occasional boat horn. He would sit for
22 hours, calmly gazing out across
23 the wide, gray river, contentedly
24 watching the birds fish and the
25 flotsam and jetsam drift silently
26 by below.

27 During the summer that Jake
28 turned 16, he had the opportunity
29 to travel with his parents on an
30 archaeological dig. They were out
31 of town for three months. When
32 they returned, Jake went straight
33 to his beloved piers. He discovered,
34 to his dismay, that they were being
35 dismantled. Little remained. Instead,

36 he came face to face with a large, official-looking sign that announced the
37 coming of a new urban park, with ball fields, pathways, fountains, benches,
38 gazebos, and kayak rentals. His riverside neighborhood, Jake saw, was
39 getting a facelift; it was getting refurbished to be safer, more attractive, and
40 family-friendly.

Name _____ Date _____

Jake's Piers

▶ **Answer each question. Give evidence from the story.**

1 What did Jake like best about the piers?

○ A. They were very near to his new home.

○ B. They provided a peaceful spot where he could sit and think undisturbed.

○ C. They had historic uses that captured his imagination.

○ D. They offered a good perch for fishing and bird-watching.

What evidence in the text helped you answer? _____

_____

_____

2 Explain how to use prefixes, suffixes, and Greek or Latin roots to determine the meaning of *inaudible* (line 19).

_____

_____

_____

3 Jake's neighborhood is "getting a facelift" (line 39). Explain the meaning of this metaphor.

_____

_____

4 What do you think *flotsam and jetsam* (line 25) are? _____

_____

_____

5 What is Jake's reaction to seeing changes along the waterfront? What does it reveal about him?

_____

_____

6 Why does the author describe the old piers as "sad and silent" (line 15)? _____

_____

_____

_____

Name _____ Date _____

Use Your Head

How does the title reflect the theme of this narrative?

1 Can a pithy remark proffered at the right time cause you to rethink
2 your view on something or even change your ways? Maybe it's a pointed
3 comment a teacher writes on one of your essays, or something brief and
4 unexpected that a friend points out.
5 There I was with my class, plodding through a modern art museum
6 along the Mall in Washington, D.C. I admit that I was bored and beat,
7 ready to return to our hotel to relax before dinner. I'd looked forward to this
8 class trip—mostly for the chance to see our nation's capital and to spend
9 time with my friends out of the classroom. I had no particular expectations
10 other than having tired feet and insufficient time to text.
11 This was our second museum of the day. We'd been slogging along for
12 hours already, and the entire group was noticeably dragging. So when Mr.
13 Soriano suggested a brief detour to the museum's ground-floor souvenir
14 shop before boarding the bus back to our hotel, I know I wasn't the only
15 one who felt relieved.
16 Oversized and unexpected red, black, and white posters bombarded us
17 from all sides as we rode the escalator down to the shop. It took an instant
18 to register that these posters displayed thought-provoking quotations,
19 all part of an exhibit called "Belief + Doubt." One of them, prominently
20 displayed on the wall ahead, riveted my attention. The words were
21 attributed to Malcolm X, a civil rights activist and writer in the 1960s.
22 I read his words twice and photographed them. The quotation read:

23   *Give your brain as much attention as you do your hair and you'll be*
24   *a thousand times better off.*

25 Back at the hotel that late afternoon, my roommates and I were
26 excitedly primping and preening in preparation for our dinner at a local
27 Thai restaurant. It seemed perfectly natural for a gaggle of giggling teens to
28 be doing this when I unexpectedly flashed upon Malcolm X's gentle scold:
29 *Give your brain as much attention as you do your hair…* I put down my brush,
30 walked to the window of our room, and peered at the city beyond.
31 I bet Malcolm X would agree that there is nothing wrong with wanting
32 to look your best. And I don't imagine I'll suddenly discard my brushes
33 and combs, or avoid fashion trends altogether. But I do hope that, going
34 forward, I'll remember that the most vital part of my head is what's inside
35 it. Maybe I'll spend a little less time looking in the mirror and a little more
36 time examining thoughts and ideas.

Name _____ Date _____

Use Your Head

▶ **Answer each question. Give evidence from the narrative.**

1 Which of the following is a synonym for *pithy* (line 1)?

○ A. long-winded　　○ B. unexpected　　○ C. humorous　　○ D. concise

What evidence in the text helped you answer? _____

_____

_____

2 What was the narrator looking forward to the most on this trip? _____

_____

_____

3 Assess the strength of the first paragraph of this personal narrative. _____

_____

_____

4 How does the narrator demonstrate that the Malcolm X quotation at the exhibit had an influence?

_____

_____

_____

5 Explain why the narrator describes the quotation as a "gentle scold" (line 28). _____

_____

_____

_____

6 Do you agree that Malcolm X's observation fits in an exhibit on "Belief + Doubt"? Explain.

_____

_____

_____

_____

Name _____ Date _____

Incident at Red Mountain

How does the setting impact this anecdote?

1 　　When he reached Milepost 27, he turned off U.S. Highway
2 180 and drove perhaps a quarter-mile along a rutted dirt road
3 to the trailhead parking area. As he unfolded himself from the
4 driver's seat, he paused a moment to absorb the spectacular
5 setting in which he now stood. The man was alone in the vast
6 high chaparral of north central Arizona. Characteristically,
7 the big sky was cloudless, enabling him to see for miles in
8 every direction. All around him grew squat shrub oak, sturdy
9 juniper and piñon pine, glistening cholla, hardy mesquite, and
10 spiky yucca and agave, replacing the towering pine, fir, and
11 aspen of the majestic San Francisco Peaks from which he'd just
12 descended. He could still see them—Humphreys Peak, Kendrick
13 Peak, Mount Elden and the others—in the near distance, dusty
14 green with splashes of brilliant yellow and burnt orange. They
15 all comprised the panoramic vistas of the Colorado Plateau,
16 this enormous uplifted landmass.
17 　　It was utterly peaceful there, the stark silence broken only occasionally
18 by the cawing of soaring raptors. The man could hear every step his
19 hiking boots took on the winding pebbled trail toward his goal, Red
20 Mountain. Red Mountain is a vermillion-walled cinder cone that had long
21 ago collapsed, revealing fascinating lunar-like interior walls. He reached it
22 after a 30-minute stroll and eagerly climbed up and in. There he lingered,
23 taking photos, making notes, thoroughly spellbound just by being there.
24 　　He was on the clock, so the man packed up and retraced his steps, sad
25 to leave but keen to reach his next destination—the Grand Canyon. On
26 the trail back to the car, he was in his own world when a stunning sight
27 stopped him dead in his tracks. A tingle of fear jolted him into the present.
28 He was petrified. The animal also halted, stood stone-still and stared
29 directly at him. At a distance of maybe 100 yards, it appeared about
30 the size of a small horse and looked like a dominant gray dog. But this
31 creature was no dog. With a racing heartbeat and growing trepidation,
32 the man moved slowly, cautiously, gathering rocks within his reach,
33 calculating his shrewdest move. The huge beast leaned toward him,
34 silently staring and sniffing. Then suddenly it wheeled and bolted away
35 through the underbrush.
36 　　When his pulse returned to normal, the man dropped the stones and
37 inhaled a mighty breath of relief. Only then did it occur to him that
38 the massive gray wolf, as elegant and graceful as it was powerful, was
39 as frightened of him as he was of it. The entire way back to the car he
40 considered what had just happened. Had he been in imminent danger?
41 Whether or not he was, he surely recognized how slight and unimportant
42 he was—an insignificant interloper in a magnificent wilderness.

Name _____ Date _____

Incident at Red Mountain

▶ **Answer each question. Give evidence from the anecdote.**

1 What does it mean that the man was "on the clock" (line 24)?

○ A. He worked as a watchmaker.   ○ C. He always knew what time it was.

○ B. He was trying to keep to a schedule.   ○ D. He was running late.

What evidence in the text helped you answer? _____

_____

_____

2 Why does the author describe the man as an "interloper" (line 42)? _____

_____

_____

3 What time of year was it for the man's trip? Explain. _____

_____

_____

4 Explain the factors that contributed to the man's trepidation (line 31) at that moment. _____

_____

_____

_____

5 Why didn't the wolf attack the hiker? _____

_____

_____

6 Why are so many of the natural features identified by their precise names, while the lone human remains nameless?

_____

_____

_____

_____

Name _____ Date _____

Fireside Chats With FDR

Why did FDR address the nation via Fireside Chats?

1 Like most families in America, ours had become
2 uncomfortably accustomed to tough times. The Great
3 Depression had had a stranglehold on the nation for over
4 a decade, and we, like so many others, were suffering.
5 Our savings were depleted, we had very little income, and
6 portentous events in Europe made the future seem onerous
7 and frightening. That's why Dad, Mother, Nell, and I always
8 huddled together by the wooden radio console on the evenings
9 when President Franklin D. Roosevelt would greet us with his
10 welcoming "My friends," and then address us so reassuringly.
11 We looked forward to the Fireside Chats, as they'd come to
12 be known, and gathered in our living room to listen intently
13 to them. My parents relaxed on the sagging couch. Dad
14 had our dog in his lap, as usual, and Mom was mending
15 something, as she typically did, to make it last a little longer.
16 Nell and I lay on our stomachs before them on the braided rug. We made a
17 point to be ready and never to miss a word.
18 We had heard most of the talks that the President had already given. And
19 when we listened, although we knew he was sitting at a desk in the White
20 House with a cluster of metal microphones before him, we felt as if he were
21 sitting where the radio stood and that we were the only ones he was addressing.
22 He provided concrete examples and helpful analogies so that all of us could
23 grasp the nature of the complex problems our country faced and the scope
24 of what lay ahead. He used language so plain and clear that even my little
25 sister could understand as he spoke about the banks, the drought, and the
26 sobering unemployment situation. He made comprehensible what he was doing
27 to remedy things. We listened attentively as Roosevelt described the explicit
28 dangers of fascism in Europe and, more recently, explained the progress our
29 armed forces were making to combat that bloodcurdling evil.
30 Tonight, we were again glued to the radio and to each other. The talk lasted
31 about three-quarters of an hour. The topic was upsetting, but FDR's soothing
32 baritone voice and moderate tempo calmed us. As he wound down his address,
33 the President urged us yet again to remain patient and patriotic. We stood
34 quietly and respectfully as "The Star Spangled Banner" played to conclude the
35 broadcast. As the final chord faded away, we stood silently for a long moment,
36 then hugged each other tightly.
37 This Fireside Chat heartened our family as we shared these dark and
38 disquieting times. My father asserted that the President made him feel as if he,
39 too, were participating in the complicated decision making. This broadcast,
40 like the many that had preceded it, redoubled my trust, admiration, and
41 appreciation of our country's steady leader.

25 Complex Text Passages to Meet the Common Core: Literature and Informational Texts, Grades 7–8 © 2014 by Scholastic Teaching Resources

Name _____ Date _____

Fireside Chats With FDR

▶ **Answer each question. Give evidence from the story.**

1 Which of the following events is most likely to be *portentous* (line 6)?

○ A. a college entrance exam   ○ C. a saber-rattling speech by a dictator

○ B. surgery to repair a broken ankle   ○ D. a check-up with the orthodontist

What evidence in the text helped you select your answer? _____

_____

_____

2 Why did President Franklin D. Roosevelt give Fireside Chats? _____

_____

_____

3 Explain why the family was "glued to the radio and to each other" (line 30). _____

_____

_____

_____

4 What does the author reveal about the family and its circumstances? Explain. _____

_____

_____

_____

5 How would you explain the family's behavior during and after the playing of "The Star-Spangled Banner"?

_____

_____

_____

6 What connects the radio with a fireplace? Explain. _____

_____

_____

Name _____ Date _____

Squishy Foam

How is the data provided for the recipe organized in a useful way?

1 ## Make-at-Home Squishy Foam

2 Be a confident kitchen chemist and cause a controlled chemical reaction to
3 create a sticky but flexible molding substance.

4 **Materials**   **Tools**

5 $\frac{1}{4}$ cup sodium borate (borax)   rubber gloves
6 3 cups cold water   assorted measuring cups
7 $1\frac{1}{2}$ cups white liquid glue   2 glass mixing bowls
8 $1\frac{1}{2}$ cups cold water   2 wooden mixing spoons
9 Food coloring
10 8 cups 3mm-polystyrene beads
11 4-gallon plastic bag (wastebasket liner size)

12 **Steps**

13 **1.** Wear rubber gloves to protect both hands. Do not remove them until you have
14 finished making the foam.

15 **2.** In a small bowl, mix the borax into 3 cups of water. Stir carefully with one of
16 the spoons until the borax is completely dissolved.

17 **3.** In the other small bowl, combine the white glue with $1\frac{1}{2}$ cups of water. Using
18 the other spoon, mix until thoroughly blended. Then add food coloring, drop-
19 by-drop, to the diluted glue to create your desired color. Mix completely.

20 **4.** Pour the glue solution into the plastic bag, then add the polystyrene beads.
21 Next, add the borax solution.

22 **5.** Holding the bag by its sides and bottom, knead together the ingredients until
23 they transform into a gummy, viscous foam. (The borax and the polyvinyl
24 acetate molecules in the glue cause a chemical reaction, creating an entirely
25 new substance—a malleable polymer foam.)

26 **6.** Remove the newly-created foam from the bag. Next, mold it into anything
27 you like, allowing it to air-dry and harden completely when you are done.
28 Alternatively, you can seal your squishy foam in a plastic bag and refrigerate it
29 for use at a later time; it will remain flexible and mold-free for several days.

Name _____ Date _____

Squishy Foam

▶ **Answer each question. Give evidence from the science recipe.**

1 Assuming one follows the directions accurately, a "controlled chemical reaction" (line 2) is most likely to be _____.

○ A. challenging ○ B. explosive ○ C. harmless ○ D. flexible

What evidence in the text helped you answer? _____

_____

_____

2 What material in the recipe is used to dilute the white glue? Explain. _____

_____

_____

3 Why are the steps numbered, but the materials and tools lists are not? _____

_____

_____

_____

4 Name two common substances that have a *viscous* (line 23) consistency. Consult a dictionary, as needed.

_____

_____

_____

5 Step 5 has a sentence set within parentheses. Why did the writer do that? _____

_____

_____

_____

6 Speculate why the author specifies using glass bowls and wooden spoons rather than bowls or spoons made of any other materials.

_____

_____

_____

Name _____ Date _____

Please Re-Boot

What elements in this business letter make it effective?

1	Customer Service Department
2	Boot Warehouse
3	500 Union Street
4	La Grande, OR 97850
5	October 13, 2013
6	To whom it may concern:
7	I recently ordered from your website a pair of well-priced, attractive, waterproof
8	rainboots, which arrived on Saturday. I selected style 13-488RB, in size 7. They arrived
9	by the date promised, they seemed to be the proper size, and complemented my
10	raincoat. However, I must report my surprise and disappointment in how the boots fit
11	when I walked outside.
12	I commute by foot to and from my job every day, a round trip of approximately 1.8 miles.
13	I live in a rainy climate, so I rely on sturdy wet-weather gear. When I wore my new boots
14	for the first time to and from my job yesterday, I found myself struggling. After walking
15	about five minutes, my feet were bone-dry but uncomfortable in other ways. The insoles
16	of both boots kept sliding up behind my heels as I walked. They slid up a bit more with
17	each step. As a result, my feet rested directly against the lumpy rubber bottoms, which
18	were cold. I developed blisters on both feet and at the back of my left heel.
19	After I arrived at work, I attempted to use glue and double-sided tape to fasten the
20	insoles into their proper place, but neither method worked. Unfortunately, I experienced
21	the same problem on my walk home.
22	I request authorization to return the boots for a full refund. I did wear them to and from
23	my job that one day, but that was the only time I wore them outside. Alas, it took an
24	actual walk in real conditions to reveal the problem I have described.
25	You will find a record of order #BNJ1950518L under my name and address. I realize that
26	I may have to pay the shipping costs to return the boots to you, but I hope you'll stand by
27	your claim of 100% customer satisfaction. Thank you.
28	Yours truly,
29	*Raven Reynolds*
30	Raven Reynolds
31	P.O. Box 87, Bluff Road
32	Klickitat, WA 98628

Name _____ Date _____

Please Re-Boot

▶ **Answer each question. Give evidence from the letter.**

1 Which has nearly the same meaning as *complemented* (line 9)?

○ A. praised   ○ B. perfected   ○ C. substituted for   ○ D. went well with

What evidence in the text helped you answer? _____

_____

_____

2 Summarize the problem Raven has with her new boots. _____

_____

_____

_____

3 Describe the structure Raven uses to organize her letter. _____

_____

_____

4 How do the form and word choice in this letter differ from those in a friendly letter? _____

_____

_____

_____

5 Why does Raven mention that she wore the boots outside and also tried to fix them herself?

_____

_____

6 Based on the letter's tone, style, and content, would you expect it to persuade Boot Warehouse to refund Raven's money? Explain.

_____

_____

_____

Name _____ Date _____

Considering Competition

Should competition play a role in the American Dream?

1   Americans thrive on competition. We enthusiastically devote time, energy, and
2 money following numerous sports in individual and team settings, with both
3 professional and amateur contenders. We play along with game shows and contests
4 on television or online. We even attempt self-improvement competitively. Does this
5 drive to be Number One reveal something about the American character?

6   **Historical Connections** Many Americans aspire to ideals collectively described
7 as the American Dream. This dream holds that liberty and freedom offer citizens
8 of every stripe an opportunity to achieve success and prosperity through hard
9 work. It is linked to that unspecified but irresistible "pursuit of happiness" our
10 founders wrote into the Declaration of Independence. Is there a connection between
11 competition and the pursuit of happiness?
12   Charles Darwin theorized that survival goes to the fittest. Is the ultimate pursuit
13 of happiness the ability to survive? Most competitions don't have stakes anywhere
14 near that severe. But do extreme competitions reveal a different, darker side to the
15 American Dream?
16   As far back as anthropologists can determine, societies and cultures have
17 typically held games and competitions. Americans have invented and celebrated
18 contests of amazing diversity. Consider these events: hot-dog-eating contests, lawn
19 mower races, rubber-ducky regattas, air-guitar championships, a paper wedding
20 gown contest, even the National Hollering Contest! When does a healthy dose of
21 competitiveness morph into a gloomy, even dangerous, obsession?

22   **Adversity** I recently saw a documentary film in which 24 adults vied to see who
23 could keep at least one hand on a brand-new pickup truck for the longest time.
24 The last one standing—without leaning on the truck or squatting—would win. This
25 outdoor contest lasted for three grueling days and nights until the winner emerged.
26 Was it worth all that agony to get something for free? According to the contestants,
27 the competition itself was the best part.

28   **Pop-Culture Trend?** A 21st-century trend in American pop culture is to televise
29 contests that promise a winner-take-all grand prize. Contestants of disparate
30 backgrounds agree to perform rigorous, often ridiculous, challenges, many of which
31 are nearly impossible for the average person. Yet viewers by the millions follow
32 these shows, vote for their favorites, argue the results, and demand more.

33   **A Distorted Dream?** Perhaps all people enjoy contests because, theoretically,
34 anybody can win. That's the American Dream right there. And perhaps each of us
35 is hard-wired to compete for what we want or need. But don't extreme contests and
36 competitions take a toll on those who participate, as well as on their rabid fans?
37 Enduring physical and mental hardships, plus shame or ridicule, may leave players
38 worse off than they were at the start. I hope we haven't belittled the American
39 Dream by recasting it as outrageous grabs at cheap glory.

Name _____ Date _____

Considering Competition

▶ **Answer each question. Give evidence from the essay.**

1 Which is the best antonym for the word *disparate* (line 29)?

○ A. comparable ○ B. dissimilar ○ C. spirited ○ D. various

What evidence in the text helped you answer? _____

_____

_____

2 Summarize the concern the writer explores in this essay. _____

_____

_____

3 Why does the author include so many questions is this essay, including the last two subheadings?

_____

_____

4 Do you think the author regards all competition as dangerous? Explain. _____

_____

_____

_____

5 The author suggests the existence of "the American character" (line 5). Is there such a thing? If so, how would you describe it?

_____

_____

_____

6 Consider competitions you know of. Describe one that the author would find harmless, and another that the author would likely find distressing. Justify your choices.

_____

_____

_____

Name _____ Date _____

Backstage at Theater Camp

What does this letter reveal about Iris and Jamie?

1   July 27, 2014

2   Oh Jamie,

3   I'm starving on the horrible prison food they serve us here, which is
4   worse than inedible. Not that I expected gourmet fare, but I swear that
5   Chewy had better food in his bowl today than I did. I'm like, "Where's Mom's
6   delectable eggplant parmesan?" So here I sit in my bunk at midday break,
7   stuffing raisins into my mouth by the fistful.

8   Two weeks into this theater-camp experience and I'm beginning to
9   wonder why I ever pestered my cheapskate parental units to send me
10 here. To be fair, some kids here are basically okay. I've even met a couple of
11 girls I imagine even you'd like. My counselor Tiffani is generally awesome.
12 She's not only writing a play when she's not supervising us, she is double-
13 jointed and can tuck her leg behind her head! Once I'm away from Tiffani
14 and my bunkmates, things plummet downhill. I'm talking about the acting
15 workshops and classes, the reasons for my presence here in the artistic
16 wilderness of northern Wisconsin.

17   Dis. A. Point. Ment! There simply aren't enough classes. I was hoping
18 for more voice lessons, dance lessons, breathing-technique coaching,
19 and improv classes—the kinds of things I'll need on that bumpy road to
20 Broadway and international fame. Seriously, I expected real challenges and
21 blunt but constructive criticism. I'd hoped to learn something tangible here
22 that I'd remember forever. But I'm not getting that, or not enough of it,
23 in any event.

24   Although we have counselors who appear to know what they're doing,
25 they focus much of their attention on the divas-in-training. (Yes, there are
26 kids here who have awesome talents and are painfully aware of it.) You of
27 all people know how much I adore performing on stage, but I feel no further
28 along skill-wise than I was when the camp session started. I honestly
29 think I've learned more about acting by watching my brother weasel his
30 way out of doing chores. I've got two more weeks here, Jamie, but I'm not
31 particularly optimistic. Unless things get into high gear, 14 days won't pass
32 quickly enough.

33   Back to my raisins.

34 Miss you,

35 Iris

Name _____ Date _____

Backstage at Theater Camp

▶ **Answer each question. Give evidence from the letter.**

1 Which is *not* a theater skill that is *tangible* (line 21)?

- ○ A. successfully doing a realistic stage faint
- ○ B. knowing tricks for memorizing lines
- ○ C. feeling passionate about acting
- ○ D. being able to cry real tears on cue

How did you determine your response? _____

_____

_____

2 What did Iris hope she would accomplish at theater camp? _____

_____

_____

_____

3 What are *divas* (line 25) and how does Iris feel about the ones at camp? _____

_____

_____

_____

4 Describe the tone and style of the letter. _____

_____

_____

_____

5 What do you think is Iris's goal in the opening paragraph of her letter? _____

_____

_____

6 What does Iris's letter tell you about Jamie? Explain. _____

_____

_____

Name _____ Date _____

Tablet, Scroll, Text

What details support writing as an essential human need?

1   Language historian and scholar I.J. Gelb once said that "writing is of such
2   importance that civilization cannot exist without it." In our modern world,
3   written words appear everywhere: in books and magazines, in ads, on maps,
4   menus, and medicine labels, on the Internet, mobile devices, and even in jewelry.
5   Gelb believed that writing was intertwined with civilization. In
6   his view, it was far more than a code of sounds in an alphabet
7   or a system of idea characters.

8   **What Is Writing?** At its heart, writing is a graphical system
9   meant to enable communication and assist in recall. Writing
10 must contain graphic marks, such as letters, symbols, and
11 ideograms. These may be recorded on paper, on any durable
12 surface, or in an electronic device. Writing must be consistent
13 enough so that people other than the writer can comprehend it.

Cuneiform tablet with carved symbols

14 **History** Historians and anthropologists dispute the exact dates when writing
15 became uniform enough to serve as a reliable means of communication. Even as
16 writing emerged, few people were literate enough to read anything that others
17 had written. Clearly, writing has come a long way. So what should we conclude
18 about writing from its development from cave art painted 30,000 years ago to
19 today's blazing cyber-media?

20 **Goals of Writing** Some might say that the highest goals of writing are to
21 stimulate thought, discussion, debate, art, and aspirations. Others hold that writing
22 exists to transmit rules, laws, and beliefs, and maintain business and historical
23 records. But perhaps the relentless march from stone tablets to
24 electronic tablets and from papyrus scrolls to scrolling down computer
25 screens simply confirms how deeply humans need to communicate.
26 We rely on words. We demand the written word. And we keep revising
27 written language to keep pace with changes in our daily lives.

28 **The Digital Revolution** In the 1980s and 1990s, computers began
29 to be integrated into our culture. It worried some people that this
30 advance would bring about the end of books. Yet few worried that
31 the written word itself would vanish. They were right. We read words
32 in "regular" books and e-books. We can shop using printed catalogs
33 or on websites, both of which still include written descriptions to
34 amplify the images. The written word is alive and well.

35 **Speaking vs. Writing** Current data reports over 7,100 living
36 languages. These are languages still spoken by people anywhere
37 in the world. However, fewer than 100 languages have written systems. This
38 difference may startle at first, but may be explained by the rise of globalization
39 and its needs. There may be fewer written languages than spoken ones, but
40 writing as a vital communication tool is likely to endure.

Modern-day tablet

Name _____ Date _____

Tablet, Scroll, Text

▶ **Answer each question. Give evidence from the essay.**

1 As it is used in line 15, *uniform* most nearly means _____.

○ A. attire   ○ B. regulated   ○ C. consistent   ○ D. symmetrical

How did you determine your response? _____

_____

_____

2 The writer begins this essay with a quotation. Give two reasons why this is an effective technique.

_____

_____

_____

3 Why does the author mention cave art (line 18) in a piece about writing? _____

_____

_____

4 Use word analysis skills to explain the meaning of *globalization* (line 38). _____

_____

_____

_____

5 In what way are the two images that accompany this essay linked? Explain. _____

_____

_____

_____

6 How might globalization affect the number of written languages in our world? _____

_____

_____

_____

Name _____ Date _____

Lincoln: A Movie Review

How does the reviewer gear comments to the intended audience?

1   Friends and classmates, I've done it for you again: I've sat through a
2   long and dull movie just so you won't have to. Admittedly, I was somewhat
3   hopeful when I entered the theater, parents and popcorn in tow. Insightful
4   moviegoer and history fan that I am, I was getting ready for the Civil
5   War. I was expecting massive armies, blasting cannon, charging cavalry,
6   deafening explosions, scenes of valiant courage and appalling destruction.
7   No such luck.
8   What I saw instead was a bunch of talkative old men with silly beards,
9   unsightly wigs, odd sideburns, wearing uncomfortable clothes, and
10 yammering endlessly in one dark, dreary chamber or another. But for a
11 brief, gruesome battle scene, there was no action, none at all! Nothing
12 blows up. There are no car chases, just hours of boring banter with no
13 relief. What a snoozer.
14 Furthermore, if a goal of this movie was to teach us how government
15 can work successfully to get things done (I read grown-up reviews by so-
16 called film critics—part of my job), it didn't even do that. All I learned was
17 that passing legislation, even something as important as a Constitutional
18 Amendment banning slavery, involves trickery, arm-twisting, name-calling,
19 and bribery. If what I witnessed was an example of governing success, what
20 does governing failure look like?
21 Now, it wouldn't be fair of me to dismiss *Lincoln* altogether with a sad
22 one-star rating. I'd be remiss not to acknowledge the top-shelf performances
23 of the principal actors. The one who played the President, for instance, was
24 particularly adept at showing us a believable Abraham Lincoln, from the
25 way he looked, walked, and thought to his reedy voice. Other performances
26 were equally effective. Kudos to the casting director, costume designer, and
27 set designer; certain scenes and characters themselves strongly resembled
28 historical photographs of the period.
29 But despite the significant topic, excellent acting, and famous director,
30 this movie was B-O-R-I-N-G. I would've fallen asleep were it not for the
31 constant hollering.

32   **My rating:** ★ ★ ☆ ☆ ☆

Name _____ Date _____

Lincoln: A Movie Review

▶ **Answer each question. Give evidence from the movie review.**

1 Which of these students would be most likely to receive *kudos* (line 26)?

○ A. the one who accumulated the most absences

○ B. the one who allowed the winning goal in a soccer game

○ C. the one whose short story was published in a magazine

○ D. the one who turns in homework on time

What evidence in the text helped you answer? _____

_____

_____

2 How would you describe the tone of this review? Give examples. _____

_____

_____

_____

3 Describe how the reviewer uses exaggeration to make a point. _____

_____

_____

_____

4 In what way is this review like a persuasive essay? _____

_____

_____

5 Notice the sentence in parentheses in lines 15 and 16. What is the purpose of this technique?

_____

_____

6 What does this review reveal about the personality of its writer? _____

_____

_____

Name _____ Date _____

Turning Point

How does the writer use language to bolster the case for a national memorial?

1 By the second decade of the 20th century, the struggle for women's suffrage
2 in the United States had been going on for nearly 70 years. Frustrated by
3 the glacial pace of state-by-state efforts to win women the right to vote, two
4 suffragists, Alice Paul and Lucy Burns, had had enough. Influenced by their
5 British sisters, they began to organize protest marches. Then, in 1917, they
6 began to form groups known as Silent Sentinels.

7 These activists quietly picketed outside the White House, but were ignored at
8 first. Eventually, they began to get arrested. They were charged with "obstructing
9 free passage of the sidewalk." More than 70 of those brave women were sent to
10 the Occoquan Workhouse in Lorton, Virginia. The conditions were harsh and
11 unsanitary in that notorious prison. The women suffered abusive, inhumane
12 treatment and subsisted on maggot-infested food. Those who refused the foul
13 food were force-fed.

14 Once news of this rough handling leaked
15 out, telegrams flooded Washington. The
16 suffrage movement had reached a turning
17 point. President Woodrow Wilson bowed to
18 public opinion and acted. He introduced the
19 Susan B. Anthony Amendment, which was
20 ratified as the 19th Constitutional Amendment
21 on August 26, 1920.

22 Today, an all-volunteer organization
23 called the Turning Point Suffragist Memorial
24 Association is itself setting up shop outside the
25 White House. Its goal is to raise sufficient funds
26 to create a national memorial across the street
27 from where the Occoquan Workhouse once
28 stood. This memorial would honor the women
29 who were held there and whose plight proved
30 to be the tipping point for the long-sought
31 goal of women's suffrage. It would honor the
32 courage and sacrifices of the countless women
33 who organized, marched, petitioned, lectured,
34 and suffered to win a long-denied right that we now take for granted.

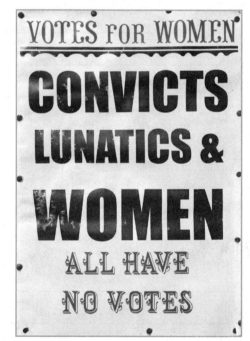

35 Across our land stand statues, monuments, and memorials honoring
36 politicians, Pilgrims, and poets. We acknowledge in stone and steel the
37 contributions of nurses, firefighters, soldiers, and sled dogs. It's high time we
38 recognize the efforts and achievements of the valiant suffragists. I applaud the
39 idea of paying tribute to them with a national memorial. I urge you to support
40 this worthy cause.

Name _____ Date _____

Turning Point

▶ **Answer each question. Give evidence from the essay.**

1 What does the author mean by referring to their *British sisters* (line 5)?

    ○ A. religious women who live and serve in Britain   ○ C. like-minded activists protesting in Britain

    ○ B. female members of the Paul and Burns families   ○ D. none of the above

How did you determine your response? _____

_____

_____

2 What prompted Alice Paul and Lucy Burns to take new action? _____

_____

_____

3 Explain what the writer means by a *tipping point* (line 30). _____

_____

_____

4 Why were the arrested protesters known as *Silent Sentinels* (line 6)? _____

_____

_____

5 Give three examples of the writer's use of highly-charged words to persuade readers of the importance of honoring the Silent Sentinels. Explain your choices.

_____

_____

_____

6 Explain the meaning of the poster. Comment on its tone and intention. _____

_____

_____

_____

Name _____ Date _____

Who Influences Young People?

How does the speaker present his/her argument?

1   Good afternoon. I've been invited to comment on today's question: *What*
2   *group of people exerts the strongest influence on the opinions of young people?* There
3   are many legitimate answers to this query. I hope that my response will shed
4   light on this subject in a manner you might not have considered.
5   Today's opening speaker named the clergy and other spiritual leaders as the
6   group that most strongly influences opinion. She claimed that because members
7   of this group enjoy a built-in following who regularly read or hear their views,
8   their influence upon young people is multiplied. I agree that this is a valid
9   point, as far as it goes. But addressing an audience of shared common values is
10 more likely to produce conformity than change.
11   The second speaker cited politicians as the group that exerts the greatest
12 influence on opinions mainly because they usually receive extensive media
13 coverage. It is inherent in their work to address the wants and needs of the
14 public, and to invite their support and feedback. But I disagree that this group
15 actually applies major influence on the opinions of our youth. Actually, I
16 suggest that most young people are less politically involved than politicians
17 might hope.
18   The speaker who represented a parent-teacher organization argued
19 passionately that the greatest influencers of youth opinions are a student's
20 family and friends, followed closely by the most effective teachers and mentors
21 in that youth's life. My own views hew most closely to this opinion. I readily
22 acknowledge the powerful impact some of my own teachers and family
23 members have had on my views, especially as I was coming of age.
24   Now to my answer. I believe that creative artists are the group that has the
25 greatest influence on young minds. I contend that public opinion changes idea
26 by idea, little by little, from the inside out. Since works of art in every medium
27 can be so rich with emotional power, their impact can be enormous. They cause
28 each participant to give something of him- or herself to connect with the work
29 and internalize its messages. Artistic works, which emerge from innovative
30 inspirations and open points of view, serve as keys that unlock the eyes, ears,
31 hearts, and minds of audiences of all ages and attitudes. The power of music
32 can transcend language and culture to evoke deep responses. Writers and poets
33 use the power of precise words and bold imagery to guide readers and listeners
34 to examine an idea in unexpected and influential ways. And visual artists—by
35 their choice of subjects in paintings, sculptures, photographs, or collages—prod
36 viewers to observe the world anew.
37   Chinese artist Ai Weiwei said, "The world is changing. This is a fact. Artists
38 work hard hoping to change it according to their own aspirations." Artists can
39 express their views without having to argue or present a thesis. A potent image
40 can demand that viewers ask questions, seek answers, and reach out to help
41 create a better world. Thank you for your attention.

Name _____ Date _____

Who Influences Young People?

▶ **Answer each question. Give evidence from the speech.**

1 This speaker is participating in a panel discussion aimed at a particular group. Who is most likely to be in the audience?

◯ A. law-enforcement officers   ◯ C. guidance counselors

◯ B. health-care professionals   ◯ D. political candidates

How did you determine your response? _____

_____

_____

2 Summarize the speaker's answer to the question stated in the opening paragraph. _____

_____

_____

_____

3 Explain what you think it means to "internalize [a] message" (line 29). _____

_____

4 What about an image might make it *potent* (line 39)? Explain. _____

_____

_____

5 Analyze the construction of this speech. Do you think it is effective? Why? _____

_____

_____

_____

6 Reread the quotation by Ai Weiwei (lines 37 and 38). Do you agree or disagree with his view? Explain.

_____

_____

_____

_____

Name _____ Date _____

Perk-Up!

What do you learn from the parts of an advertisement?

1 Shayna spotted this online advertisement for a new soft drink now appearing on
2 drug store, supermarket, and health food store shelves in select areas.

3 **Do you need**
4 **an energy boost**
5 **to begin your**
6 **mornings?**

7 **Are you tired**
8 **of the same-old**
9 **sports drinks that**
10 **taste like year-old**
11 **lollipops?**

12 **Are you looking**
13 **for a beverage**
14 **that will whet your whistle while**
15 **jump-starting your engine?**

16 **If so, then come join the thousands**
17 **of satisfied Americans who now start their**
18 **day with a frosty glass of Perk-Up!**

19 **This exciting new beverage contains**
20 **20% *real* fruit juice!**

21 **Trainers and health-care professionals**
22 **heartily agree that Perk-Up works best to**
23 **keep you fit!**

24 **Nutrition and content labels present the**
25 **required information about the contents**
26 **of each bottle of Perk-Up.**

NUTRITION FACTS

Serving Size 8 fl oz (240 mL)
Servings per container   4

Amount per Serving	
Calories 175	
	% Daily Value
Total Fat 0g	0%
Cholesterol 0mg	0%
Sodium 70 mg	2%
Total Carbohydrate 2g	24%
Sugars 68g	
Fiber 0g	
Protein 0g	0%

Vitamin A	10%	Vitamin C	100%
Calcium	0%	Iron	0%

CONTAINS 20% juice

INGREDIENTS: water, high-fructose corn syrup, concentrated apple juice, citric acid, concentrated guava and pineapple juice, xanthan gum, sodium citrate, ascorbic acid, gum acacia, citrus oils, other natural flavors, artificial colors

Name _____ Date _____

Perk-Up!

▶ **Answer each question. Give evidence from the advertisement.**

1 Which daily nutritional need would Perk-Up best fulfill?

○ A. fiber   ○ B. protein   ○ C. vitamin C   ○ D. carbohydrates

How did you determine your response? _____

_____

_____

2 Could you purchase Perk-Up anywhere? Explain. _____

_____

_____

3 What is the capacity of a container of Perk-Up? Tell how you figured it out. _____

_____

_____

4 Read the ingredients list. Why do you think that water is listed first? _____

_____

5 How does the photograph support the ad? _____

_____

_____

_____

6 Some advertising can intentionally mislead. Read the ad copy carefully and with skepticism.
Pose four questions you could ask about the claims made.

_____

_____

_____

_____

_____

_____

Name _____ Date _____

GMO: Yes or No?

How does the author illuminate a complex topic?

1 Have you heard of *frankenfoods*? Even if you haven't, you probably
2 can picture the monster created by Dr. Frankenstein in the 1818 classic
3 novel by Mary Shelley. Shelley's so-called mad scientist experimented
4 to bring life to a human cadaver by charging it with electricity. The
5 monster came to life. But lacking understanding of the world, it
6 terrorized the local village and brought shame to Dr. Frankenstein.
7 Some people use the derogatory term *frankenfood* to describe any food
8 product that contains ingredients that were scientifically engineered in some
9 way to change their original properties. This term suits the deeply skeptical views
10 of this camp, who hope to frighten people away from such foods. Yet supporters
11 of genetic engineering suggest that improvements to plants can one day help end
12 world hunger. How can two such divergent views co-exist?
13 Genetic engineering is a process that isolates a specific gene from one
14 organism and inserts it into a different organism, called the host. The goal is for
15 the desired trait in the transferred gene to become part of the host organism's
16 new-and-improved gene structure for some advantage. Some plants, for example,
17 can resist the compounds in pesticides that harm insects. This results in sturdier
18 crops. Engineered corn can produce a substance within it that makes the corn
19 resist pests, thus eliminating the need to apply pesticides at all. "Golden rice" has
20 been engineered to contain extra vitamin A, an essential nutrient that is lacking
21 in many rice-based diets.
22 Many genetic changes to living things have occurred naturally over time.
23 Adaptations help an organism withstand environmental challenges. For
24 instance, desert plants evolved to require far less water than other plants so they
25 can withstand arid conditions. Some coastal plants, such as the mangrove, have
26 evolved to be able to survive on salt water.
27 For generations, farmers grafted plants together to create better new plants.
28 A common example of this is the lemon. Scientists suggest that the lemon derived
29 from a cross between a sour orange and a citron. Also, wise farmers would save
30 seeds from one year's best crops in hopes that the next year's yield from those
31 seeds would be even better. This sort of natural tinkering was thought to benefit
32 our diets and has been widely accepted.
33 But now there are new concerns. Thanks to advances in scientific
34 understanding of genetics, combined with the availability of high-tech
35 equipment for laboratory manipulation, the safety of altered plants comes into
36 question. Opponents of frankenfoods argue that changing the genetic material
37 in one organism can adversely affect the entire food chain. They also believe that
38 food engineered to resist one problem may, over time, cause another, perhaps
39 worse one. They fear a terrible chain-reaction that would affect our ability to feed
40 ourselves, remain healthy, and protect our planet.
41 Do any of the foods you consume contain GMOs (genetically modified
42 organisms)? Would you know if they did? Would it concern you?

Name _____ Date _____

GMO: Yes or No?

▶ **Answer each question. Give evidence from the essay.**

1 Someone who holds *skeptical* (line 9) views would likely be _____.

○ A. easy to fool   ○ B. suspicious   ○ C. a fussy eater   ○ D. trusting

How did you determine your response? _____

_____

_____

2 What is the writer's goal in the opening paragraph of the piece? _____

_____

_____

_____

3 Explain how the picture reflects views about genetically modified foods. _____

_____

_____

4 State the main concern opponents raise about genetically modified foods. _____

_____

_____

_____

5 What is unusual about the closing paragraph? What might be the writer's purpose in ending this way?

_____

_____

6 What clues in this essay indicate that it was written to inform rather than persuade? _____

_____

_____

_____

_____

Name _____ Date _____

Letter of Application

What can you learn about a writer from a personal essay?

1   April 4, 2013

2   To whom it may concern:

3   I am applying for entrance to the High School for Math and Science in the fall
4   of 2013. I have thoroughly researched the rich offerings at your school and am
5   eager to be part the next freshman class.

6   I have always loved mathematics, particularly statistics. Since I was a child,
7   I have studied baseball stats intensely, including the sophisticated kind of
8   statistical analysis called sabermetrics, first introduced by Bill James about 35
9   years ago. Although, unlike my brothers, I am not much of an athlete, I have
10   been fascinated with reading, memorizing, analyzing, and making predictions
11   from team and individual player data. In fact, I have developed my own
12   algorithm for evaluating players' batting prospects. One day, I hope to pursue
13   a career in statistics, not necessarily as it relates to sports, but perhaps in its
14   application to politics, economics, or business. I look forward to continuing
15   my study of advanced math, particularly the applied math, engineering, and
16   science classes your school offers.

17   I enjoy science as much as I enjoy math, and study hard to grasp and apply
18   the concepts I have been learning. Here, for you to peruse, is a table comparing
19   my grades on our four most recent science tests with those of three classmates
20   also applying to your school. (I have omitted their names.)

21   I truly love school and
22   study hard. Furthermore, I like
23   sharing what I know to help
24   my classmates. For instance,
25   I currently volunteer as a peer
26   math and science tutor after
27   school two days each week.
28   I hope to continue doing so in
29   high school.

	Test 1	Test 2	Test 3	Test 4	Mean	Median
Myself	95	90	100	95	95	95
Peer A	95	85	85	90	87.5	87.5
Peer B	85	80	80	80	81.25	80
Peer C	80	90	90	75	83.75	85

30   But please don't envision me
31   as one-dimensional. Some of
32   my other interests include jewelry making, tap dancing, blogging, and playing
33   classical music. My mother is a jewelry maker, and my father is a pianist. I am
34   studying the viola, and hold the first chair in my school's chamber orchestra.

35   To conclude, let me reiterate how much I want to attend your school. I believe
36   it is the right place for me, and I assert that I am the right person for you. I so
37   look forward to walking through your doors next September. Please give me the
38   chance. Thank you.

39   Respectfully yours,
40   Eleni Vasilakis

Name _____ Date _____

Letter of Application

▶ **Answer each question. Give evidence from the letter.**

1 Which means the same as *peer*, as it is used in the table and in line 25?

○ A. wharf   ○ B. examiner   ○ C. colleague   ○ D. aristocrat

What evidence in the text helped you answer? _____

_____

2 Summarize why Eleni hopes to attend the High School for Math and Science. _____

_____

_____

_____

3 Why do you think Eleni includes non-academic interests in her letter? _____

_____

_____

4 Why did Eleni include a data table? Do you find this an effective strategy? Explain. _____

_____

_____

_____

5 Which part of Eleni's letter do you find the weakest? What changes might you suggest? _____

_____

_____

_____

6 Write a brief character sketch of Eleni Vasilakis based on how she presents herself in her personal essay.

_____

_____

_____

_____

Name _____ Date _____

Fine Art vs. Folk Art

How does the author motivate, inform, and persuade readers?

1   The mission of a museum is to preserve,
2 display, and explain the value of the works
3 in its collection. So why do some visitors feel
4 intimidated by certain works? Do museums
5 attempt to define what art should be? It's
6 a fair question that deserves a thoughtful
7 response.
8   Art historians and museum curators are
9 generally well-educated people who immerse
10 themselves in their subject. So why do they
11 often ignore an entire category of art? Let's
12 first define two distinct groups of artwork.
13   Fine (or academic) art is what's found
14 in museums, art books, and grand public
15 spaces. It becomes legitimate mainly by
16 its connections to academic institutions.

Detail from a
hand-carved bench

17 Most fine artists attended universities or art
18 schools to develop their skills under the watchful eyes of instructors. By
19 contrast, folk art is the product of self-taught creative people who work
20 outside such institutions. Folk artists typically bring their experiences
21 to their work, art that can be naïve, ornamental, functional, spiritual,
22 dramatic, but not necessarily pleasing to the aesthete's eye. Folk art
23 may ignore classic rules of perspective or proportion and rarely follows
24 academic trends.
25   If the purpose of art is to express one's creative vision through work
26 in a chosen medium, then shouldn't folk art be just as valid as fine art?
27 Perhaps these two styles need not compete since each style displays unique
28 elements that demonstrate its value. Moreover, they also share many
29 fundamental attributes.
30   All artists express their cultural identities and convey their values and
31 traditions. They may work in any medium—fabric, wood, clay, paper,
32 metals, plastics, paints, chalk, pencil, stone, glass—to create paintings,
33 sculptures, pottery, furniture, and decorative or functional items. Why
34 compare Picasso and Grandma Moses?
35   In 1971, Edgar Tolson, a Kentucky folk artist, may have captured the
36 essence of art when he said, "You don't make it with your hands. You form
37 it with your hands. You make it with your mind."
38   It may be time for museums, galleries, and other art institutions to
39 make space on their walls for art from every noteworthy source. Such an
40 approach could show visitors a greater range of creative possibilities to
41 help them better appreciate the diverse ways artists dare to explore.

Name _____ Date _____

Fine Art vs. Folk Art

▶ **Answer each question. Give evidence from the essay.**

1 Which two words from the essay have nearly the same meaning?

○ A. *academic* (line 13) and *fundamental* (line 29)   ○ C. *perspective* (line 23) and *attributes* (line 29)

○ B. *distinct* (line 12) and *classic* (line 23)   ○ D. *legitimate* (line 15) and *valid* (line 26)

How did you determine your response? _____

_____

_____

2 Based on the essay, summarize the main difference between fine art and folk art. _____

_____

_____

_____

3 Why does the writer contend that folk art is an authentic art form? _____

_____

_____

_____

4 What does a museum *curator* (line 8) do? Consult a reference as needed. _____

_____

_____

5 Paraphrase Edgar Tolson's statement (lines 36–37) in your own words. _____

_____

_____

6 Examine the image that accompanies the essay. Do you think it represents fine art, folk art, or both?
Explain.

_____

_____

_____

Name _____ Date _____

Proposition 43

How does the editorial make its case to readers?

1   Our state's professional football
2   team seeks a new stadium.
3   Our local urban planning
4   commission is considering their
5   request to construct it right here
6   in City Center. Proposition 43 on
7   the November ballot will ask you
8   to vote for or against this plan.
9   Knowing that our citizens will
10 have to bear a sizable portion
11 of the hefty cost, and that there
12 will be problems both known and
13 unknown, we are firmly against
14 the plan. We think that building
15 a huge football stadium in the
16 heart of our already crowded
17 and busy city would be a grave
18 mistake.

19 **Good Business?** Those in favor
20 of the new site say that placing
21 a stadium here is good business.
22 They claim that it will create
23 jobs and boost the economy
24 by adding new businesses
25 like hotels, restaurants, and
26 souvenir shops. They add that
27 having a team right here in
28 our city would be a big morale
29 booster and would bring people
30 together. Team representatives
31 and their associates in the
32 construction industry are busy
33 lobbying for this project. Do not
34 underestimate them.

35 **On the Other Hand . . .**
36 Admittedly, there could be
37 some positives to their plans.
38 But constructing a 75,000-seat

39 complex in the middle of an
40 already congested city would
41 be far more trouble than it's
42 worth. For one thing, additional
43 traffic will create bottlenecks
44 and gargantuan transportation
45 problems. Secondly, having a
46 stadium here would be very bad
47 for the community; the rowdy,
48 noisy crowds would fill the
49 streets, bringing disruption and
50 leaving garbage, which would
51 be unsanitary at best, dangerous
52 at worst. Furthermore, the cost
53 would be prohibitive. We think
54 that the city and its taxpayers
55 would be better served spending
56 money to build needed housing,
57 upgrade neglected parks,
58 improve city-wide school facilities
59 or public transportation, or fix
60 our pot-holed roads, wobbling
61 bridges, and deteriorating
62 tunnels. Work on any of these
63 alternatives would do as much or
64 more for our economic well-being
65 as would the construction of a
66 stadium.

67 **Vote** There are powerful interests
68 behind the plan to build in
69 City Center, but their interest is
70 mainly self-interest. Carefully
71 considering the pros and cons of
72 such a colossal undertaking, we
73 believe that the negatives greatly
74 outweigh the positives. Our city
75 is the wrong location for the new
76 stadium. We urge you to vote NO
77 on Proposition 43.

Name _____ Date _____

Proposition 43

▶ **Answer each question. Give evidence from the editorial.**

1 Which of the following is *not* an argument the developers use to support building a new football stadium in City Center?

○ A. The stadium will improve traffic flow.   ○ C. A pro team in the city will boost morale.

○ B. The stadium will provide needed jobs.   ○ D. New businesses will energize the economy.

What evidence in the text helped you answer? _____

_____

_____

2 Who is the "we" (lines 13, 14, 53, 76) the writer refers to in this editorial? _____

_____

3 In your view, which is the editorial's strongest argument against building the new stadium? Explain.

_____

_____

_____

4 Use word analysis skills to explain the meaning of *prohibitive* as it is used in the sentence in line 53.

_____

_____

5 In line 70, the editorial accuses the supporters of the new stadium of self-interest. Explain the writer's concern.

_____

_____

_____

6 How is the editorial's closing paragraph related to its opening? Explain. _____

_____

_____

_____

Name _____   Date _____

Launch, Circuit, Land

How does the title fit the passage?

1   The history of aviation is replete with famous pioneers whose
2   vision, courage, and endurance broke barriers. The list is long
3   and storied, from the Montgolfier brothers of France and their
4   first hot-air balloon flights in 1783 to Yuri Gagarin, the first
5   human to orbit the earth in 1961. More recently, the allure of
6   flight has attracted younger participants who long to spread
7   their wings and take to the skies.
8   Callum Lavender of the United Kingdom was 13 years old
9   when he learned that the minimum legal age for solo glider
10 pilots would soon be lowered from 16 to 14. So he began taking
11 lessons, encouraged by his father, already an experienced glider
12 pilot. In fact, Callum's dad was at the controls when the seven-
13 year-old boy experienced his first glider flight. Over the years,
14 as they soared together, Mr. Lavender taught his son as much as
15 he could. But both Lavenders acknowledged that any pilot who
16 hopes to fly solo must undertake formal instruction, including
17 rigorous safety training.
18   So Callum began weekly training lessons at Bicester Flight
19 Centre, near his home. His instructor, Alan Smith, claims that the teen took to
20 gliding like a duck to water. "Teaching young people is always a joy, and in
21 Callum's case, he absorbed all the knowledge like a sponge," Smith remembers.
22 Fourteen weeks later, Callum became certified to make his first solo glider flight.
23 It was planned for the day of his fourteenth birthday.
24   But when the big day arrived, unfavorable weather conditions grounded
25 Callum. Though disappointed, he knew that safety was the utmost concern,
26 so he found the patience to wait out the bad weather. Two days later, Callum
27 Lavender successfully made his initial solo flight, soaring about a thousand feet
28 above the countryside. According to the British Gliding Association, he became
29 the nation's youngest solo glider pilot.
30   Meanwhile, on the ground, Judith
31 Lavender admitted her anxiety over her
32 son's goal. "I was absolutely terrified,"
33 she confessed. "For three months I
34 watched him go up in a glider, but
35 he always had an experienced and
36 competent instructor in the back seat."
37 But Callum took the experience in
38 stride. "Before the flight I was scared,
39 but as soon as I got up there it all
40 clicked into a routine flight," he recalls.
41 "Launch, circuit, land."

Are gliders airplanes?

Like airplanes, gliders can soar through the air under the control of an experienced pilot. But they lack engines, so they cannot take off on their own. Gliders are designed to have a lightweight fuselage and very long wings.

25 Complex Text Passages to Meet the Common Core: Literature and Informational Texts, Grades 7–8 © 2014 by Scholastic Teaching Resources

Name _____ Date _____

Launch, Circuit, Land

▶ **Answer each question. Give evidence from the passage.**

1 Why did Callum begin to take formal flying lessons (line 16)?

○ A. His mother insisted because she feared for his safety.

○ B. Solo pilots must get certified by an instructor.

○ C. It was the only way Callum could get flight time.

○ D. His father's knowledge was not good enough.

How did you determine your response? _____

_____

2 Rewrite the opening sentence of the piece, keeping its exact meaning but without using the word *replete*.

_____

_____

3 Why does the author use the expression "spread their wings" (lines 6 and 7)? Describe a deeper meaning of this expression.

_____

_____

4 What does this passage reveal about Callum's parents? _____

_____

_____

5 Read the sidebar text and examine the photo. What is a *fuselage*, and why would a glider fuselage have to be lightweight?

_____

_____

6 Based on this biographical sketch, what careers might Callum pursue as an adult? Support your predictions with evidence from the text.

_____

_____

_____

Name _____   Date _____

Miracle on Ice

What turned an ice hockey game into a sports history milestone?

1 "Do you believe in miracles?" asked sportscaster Al Michaels as the game
2 wound down to its final seconds. "Yes!" was his clear response as the horn
3 sounded and the delirious, raucous crowd of 8,500 hockey fans that filled the
4 Field House that day waved their flags and screamed in delight. The date was
5 February 22, 1980, during the Winter Olympics at Lake Placid, New York. The
6 cause for the pandemonium was that the underdog American ice hockey team
7 had just defeated the highly-favored Soviets, 4–3, in a medal round.

8 **Cold War Opponents** The Americans and Soviets that year were still
9 enmeshed in a decades-old cold war. As a result, their sports teams were
10 archrivals. The American hockey team was composed of both amateurs and
11 pros, including nine players from the University of Minnesota and four members
12 of the Boston University squad. The Soviet team, which had won nearly every
13 Olympic or world hockey championship during the previous quarter century,
14 was expected again to be victorious. After all, they'd won the previous four
15 Olympic gold medals, outscoring their opponents 175–44 in the process. The
16 1980 team had faster skaters than their American counterparts did, were more
17 skilled, and had the world's top goaltender.

18 **Game Time** Before the game, American coach Herb Brooks tried to elevate his
19 players' confidence. He exhorted them, "You were born to be a player. You were
20 meant to be here. This moment is yours." Then the much-anticipated game
21 began. The Americans fell behind early, tied up the game, and then fell behind
22 again. They grabbed the lead once more in the third period and then held on
23 to it ferociously for the final ten
24 minutes. The world watched in
25 disbelief, as if they had just seen
26 a high school football team beat
27 Super Bowl champs.

28 **Champions** Brooks' dazzling
29 American team went on to
30 defeat Finland to win the gold,
31 but it was the thrilling game
32 with the Soviets that grabbed
33 the headlines. That improbable
34 victory was cited by Sports
35 Illustrated in 1999 as the Top
36 Sports Moment of the 20th
37 century. It was a game known
38 forever after for what it felt like:
39 a miracle on ice.

To celebrate the Olympic-winning coach who urged his team to victory, a bronze statue of Brooks now stands in his hometown of St. Paul, Minnesota.

Name _____ Date _____

Miracle on Ice

▶ **Answer each question. Give evidence from the article.**

1 The best meaning of *exhort* (line 19) in this piece is to _____.

○ A. admonish   ○ B. caution   ○ C. advise   ○ D. urge earnestly

What evidence in the text helped you answer? _____

_____

_____

2 What made the American and Soviet hockey teams such archrivals? _____

_____

3 Judge the writer's opening paragraph. Use details to support your opinion. _____

_____

_____

_____

_____

4 In what ways does the photograph support the article? Be specific. _____

_____

_____

_____

5 How does the writer use figurative language to emphasize the unlikely outcome of the game?

_____

_____

_____

_____

6 As used in this article, is *miracle* a term to be taken literally? Explain. _____

_____

_____

Name _____ Date _____

El Sistema

How does El Sistema affect the lives of its participants?

1 Not only is music compelling to children, in the right
2 circumstances it can influence them to develop into industrious
3 and confident adults. Just ask award-winning orchestral conductor
4 Gustavo Dudamel, who now enjoys a fulfilling international
5 career. Born in a small town in Venezuela, Maestro Dudamel
6 began to study music as a boy with the now-famous *El Sistema*
7 program. El Sistema has shown how music can bring about social
8 change to improve lives. Today, four decades after its launch, El
9 Sistema sponsors more than 500 child and youth orchestras, 30
10 professional orchestras, and nearly 400 choruses at no cost to
11 participants. And El Sistema programs now thrive in almost 30 countries.

12 **Guiding Principles** El Sistema loves children first and music second. The
13 program strives to create a caring community where children at every age feel
14 both protected and challenged. Discipline and hard work are expected of each
15 participant. Yet a steady spirit of joy and purpose informs everything.

16 **"To Play and to Fight"** The motto of El Sistema—*Tocar y Luchar*—serves
17 to motivate. It is a pledge to embrace music as a powerful group experience
18 that also involves major individual effort. It requires a commitment to pursue
19 excellence. Above all, El Sistema's motto means to persist and strive until
20 dreams become reality.

21 **Instructional Routines** The music program features intensive ensemble
22 work that includes group learning, peer teaching, and regular performance
23 opportunities. Children may begin attending a local El Sistema center at age
24 2 or 3. The youngest children explore music through body movement and
25 rhythm. By age 5, the young musicians begin to sing in choirs. They also play
26 recorder and percussion instruments. By age 7, students may pick a string or
27 wind instrument to pursue. Singing, instrumental work, and reading standard
28 musical notation are developed at all levels. Weekly practice sessions, ensemble
29 work, small-group instruction, and private lessons are available to all. Students
30 routinely perform for audiences both to decrease performance anxiety and to
31 make performing a natural part of the musical experience.

32 **Summary** There can be no better summary of the enduring success and value
33 of El Sistema than this quotation taken directly from its website:

34 *Graduates leave with a sense of capability, endurance and resilience—owning a*
35 *confidence about taking on enormous challenges in their lives. A deep sense of value,*
36 *of being loved and appreciated, and a trust for group process and cooperation, enables*
37 *them to feel that excellence is in their own hands.*

Name _____ Date _____

El Sistema

▶ Answer each question. Give evidence from the article.

1 Which is *not* a reason that El Sistema participants perform frequently?

○ A. to reduce performance anxiety   ○ C. to allow individuals a chance to shine

○ B. to impress visitors and critics   ○ D. to make it a normal part of the experience

What evidence in the text helped you answer? _____

_____

_____

2 Why would the writer mention Gustavo Dudamel in the introduction? Explain. _____

_____

3 What does *inform* mean in the phrase "informs everything" (line 15)? Consult a dictionary, as needed, to determine the correct usage.

_____

_____

4 Summarize the prevailing atmosphere at an El Sistema center. _____

_____

_____

_____

5 What does the author means by stating, "El Sistema loves children first and music second" (line 12)?

_____

_____

6 The brief motto of El Sistema is explained in paragraph 3. But it suggests other implications. Analyze the motto for other levels of meaning.

_____

_____

_____

_____

Name _____ Date _____

Eccentric Family Staycation

How does the title capture the essence of the Oh family's experience?

1 When David Oh, his wife, and their three children went to be interviewed
2 on National Public Radio in California at 10:00 A.M., they knew that they'd be
3 going to sleep as soon as they returned home after the interview concluded. Oh,
4 you see, was flight director of an extraordinary adventure—tracking the Mars
5 Rover as it went about its discovery mission on the red planet. To do his job, Oh
6 and 800 other engineers and scientists had to adjust their body clocks to live on
7 Mars time here on Earth. In a unique group experiment, the rest of the Ohs also
8 shifted to Mars time to share an unprecedented and eccentric family summer
9 staycation.
10 A day on Mars is nearly 40 minutes longer than a day on Earth. By the time
11 of the interview, the Ohs had been at it for a few weeks and change, and were
12 now about half a day off Earth time. For them, 10:00 A.M. felt like 10:00 P.M. This
13 shift enabled them to lounge on the beach at midnight and bowl at 4:00 A.M.
14 The youngest child safely learned to ride a two-wheeler in an empty parking lot;
15 it was three in the morning, after all! By being awake at these odd times, the
16 whole family got the chance to observe an eye-popping meteor shower.
17 The family's new "day" required some new language. To emulate the
18 technical language of the Rover team, they called each new day a *sol*. Then
19 they turned into neologists. They called "yesterday" *yestersol*; "tomorrow night"
20 became *solmorrow* night.
21 By taking part in this singular experiment, the family got to appreciate some
22 of the unexpected demands of scientific research. They developed a deeper sense
23 of life on Mars, much more so than if they had, like the rest of us, only seen the
24 amazing photos Curiosity was transmitting back to Earth.
25 As the summer came to a close, the Oh children and their mom shifted back to
26 Earth time. They resumed their normal routines to prepare for the new school year.

	Earth	Mars
Mean distance from Sun	93 million mi	141.6 million mi
Period of revolution around Sun	365.256 days	686.98 days
Synodic day (midday to midday)	24h 0m 0s	24h 39m 35s
Mass (Earth = 1)	1	0.107
Mean radius	3958.8 mi	2106 mi
Mean density (Earth = 1)	1	0.713
Average surface temperature	59°F	−81°F

The difference in the synodic day is not the only difference between Earth and Mars. The table shows others.

Name _____ Date _____

Eccentric Family Staycation

▶ **Answer each question. Give evidence from the essay.**

1 Why is the word *Curiosity* (line 24) capitalized?

    ◯ A. It represents a secret code word.   ◯ C. It names a member of Dr. Oh's team.

    ◯ B. It is the name of the Mars Rover.   ◯ D. It is the name given to the Mars project.

What evidence in the text helped you answer? _____

_____

_____

2 What prompted the Oh family to undertake an unusual family experiment? _____

_____

_____

3 Use context clues and word study skills to determine the meaning of *neologists* (line 19). _____

_____

_____

4 Describe the characteristics of the Oh family, based on the essay. _____

_____

_____

_____

5 How were the *circadian rhythms* of the Oh family members affected by their experiment?
Use a dictionary or other resource and evidence from the text to explain. Which phrase in the essay
relates to circadian rhythms?

_____

_____

_____

6 Examine the table. Why is distance from the sun given as *mean* distance? _____

_____

_____

Literature Passages

Passage 1: Medicine Walk

1. D; Sample answer: Tyler expressed his anxiety in the thoughts running through his head (lines 1–4), but as his anxiety increases, he begins to feel a sense of shame (lines 9–10, 19–22). **2.** Sample answer: Mr. Melvin experienced his own medicine walk at about the same age and can share his concerns, reactions, and reflections. He is also patient and encouraging (lines 13–18, 23–41). **3.** Sample answer: A medicine walk is a solo outdoor experience a young person undertakes to build maturity, independence, inner-strength, and self-awareness (lines 1–22, 31–41). **4.** Sample answer: It is probably a phrase that Mr. Melvin or Tyler's parents may have used to justify this undertaking. **5.** Sample answer: I would choose the word *intimidating* in line 31. Both words mean that the task is formidable and can inspire fear and apprehension. **6.** Sample answer: He shares his own first-hand experiences, acknowledges the anxieties the boys probably feel, and provides them with hands-on practice and sensible, reassuring advice. He reminds them that they know what they need to know and that the task, while daunting, is within their ability (lines 11–18, 23–41).

Passage 2: Hakim's Workplace

1. D; Sample answer: An onomatopoeic word makes the sound associated with it. So *yipping* makes the high, piercing sound it means. **2.** Sample answer: Hakim shines shoes in a railroad station (lines 1–6, 8–12, 26–28). **3.** Sample answer: You expect certain sounds and sights in a train station every day; the author describes people coming and going, familiar sounds, routines, greetings, etc. Hakim has become attuned to these daily rhythms (lines 8–9). **4.** Sample answer: It means that he gets much of his information through his sense of hearing. **5.** Sample answer: He seems to be comfortable in and familiar with his surroundings in the train station. He is observant but doesn't get involved and carries on with his work (lines 7–28). **6.** Sample answer: The girls are excitedly racing to meet friends while their mother and younger brother hurry to keep up with them, not wanting to get separated in the crowded station.

Passage 3: The Steadfast Parrot

1. B; Sample answer: The parrot kept cool and made the best of the situation, which had changed drastically. **2.** Sample answer: To undulate means to have a wavy form; a good example from nature is an ocean wave or prairie grasses blowing in the wind. **3.** Sample answer: Shakra used his powers to test the small bird to see if she was being truthful. This made Shakra seem mean and too demanding of the bird who'd shown only affection and loyalty to the tree (lines 15–17, 30–31). **4.** Sample answer: The parrot speaks as though she is human, and expresses feelings of gratitude and freedom (lines 8–12, 26–29, 38–40). The banyan tree is said to offer hospitality, as if an actual host (lines 1–9). **5.** Sample answer: Each provides something to the other without asking for anything in return. The tree gives the parrot all that she needs; the love and gratitude the parrot feels for the banyan leads her to stay by it even in bad times. That's how close friends treat each other. **6.** Sample answer: The parrot could represent anyone loyal and true through good times and bad. When Shakra tested the parrot by destroying the banyan, he found that she didn't abandon her friend. Loyalty and gratitude are high virtues (lines 7–14, 17–29, 38–41). The lesson would be to keep promises, and stay true and loyal to your friends. These things will be rewarded (the banyan was revived).

Passage 4: Ethan Allen, Gentleman

1. B; Sample answer: I knew that the words *savvy* and *astute* both describe positive attributes of successful people in business and politics, so I chose B. **2.** Sample answer: Allen first encouraged her verbally. Then he demonstrated, by letting the dentist pull one of his teeth, that the process wasn't as bad as she feared (lines 21–38). **3.** Sample answer: The language is more formal, polite, and measured than people usually speak nowadays, so it gives it the feel of a different time of reserved manners. **4.** Sample answer: His experience probably told him that he could not save the tooth. At that time, dentistry was more primitive and painful than it is today. **5.** Sample answer: He was gallant in trying to reassure a frightened woman in pain and in coaxing her to do what was medically necessary. But he was deceitful in pretending that the extraction was painless (lines 21–24, 33–38). **6.** Sample answer: A gentleman is courteous, kind, brave, and willing to suffer or sacrifice to benefit another person, even one he barely knows (lines 21–38).

Passage 5: Jake's Piers

1. B; Sample answer: Jake went there to be "alone with his thoughts in the eerie silence" (lines 17–26). **2.** Sample answer: I know that the root *aud* is related to sound, as in *audio*. The prefix *in-* means "not" and the suffix *-able* means "can be." So, *inaudible* means "cannot be heard," which is confirmed by line 19 ("All Jake could hear as he sat…"). **3.** Sample answer: An actual facelift is a surgical way to try to improve someone's looks. In this piece, a neighborhood facelift makes the area look better and more appealing. **4.** Sample answer: I think this phrase means things that float by in the water, like leaves, sticks, or bits and pieces of old junk. **5.** Sample answer: He was dismayed that his private sanctuary would never be the same for him. I think his reaction shows that he's a private kid who likes to be left alone to ponder things and finds comfort even in a run-down abandoned structure that he can feel is his (lines 31–35). **6.** Sample answer: The piers are sad because they are no longer used, and are damaged and empty, and silent since they no longer belong to the city's vibrant life (lines 12–16).

Passage 6: Use Your Head

1. D; Sample answer: In order to change how you think, it takes a sharp comment, like a zinger (lines 1–4). **2.** Sample answer: The narrator looked forward to seeing Washington, D.C., and spending time with her friends outside the classroom (lines 7–9). **3.** Sample answer: By beginning with a thought-provoking question, the writer grabs the reader's attention and engages readers to think, right from the start (lines 1–4). **4.** Sample answer: The narrator read it twice, took a picture of it, and, back at the hotel, turned away from the mirror and gazed out at the city, lost in thought about it (lines 23–36). **5.** Sample answer: It's a gentle scold because it's not insulting and doesn't make fun of trying to look one's best, but it does make a person stop and think about how best to use his or her time (lines 23–36). **6.** Sample answer: I think it fits because if you give your brain attention, you are believing in who you are and what you think/feel rather than just how you look (lines 23–27).

Passage 7: Incident at Red Mountain

1. B; Sample answer: In lines 24–25, the author says that the man had to get to his next destination. **2.** Sample answer: He is an interloper because he is intruding upon a vast wilderness, home not to humans but to wild animals and native plants. **3.** Sample answer: It must have been the fall because the writer notes the brilliant yellow and burnt orange colors of the leaves, which change color in fall (lines 12–14). **4.** Sample answer: He was alone, far from civilization or even his car, and facing a wild wolf who was looking at him and might attack (lines 25–32). **5.** Sample answer: Maybe the wolf was as afraid of encountering a human as the man was to come across a wolf. Maybe the wolf wasn't hungry, or went to alert the rest of its pack! **6.** Sample answer: The man represents all humans, suggesting that people are merely visitors in the much larger wilderness (lines 41–42).

Passage 8: Fireside Chats With FDR

1. C; Sample answer: Because the writer says that portentous events in Europe made our future seem frightening, *portentous* could mean "bad" or "scary," I picked C (lines 1–7, 27–29). **2.** Sample answer: In the days before TV and the Internet, the president used radio broadcasts to speak directly and reassuringly to a concerned and frightened American public (lines 18–33). **3.** Sample answer: They were seeking information, encouragement, and signs of hope from a president who attempted to calm them. And in hard times they depended on each other (lines 11–29, 37–41). **4.** Sample answer: They did not have much money, as indicated by the sagging couch and the mom mending clothes to make them last longer. The author highlights their sense of togetherness as they gather around the radio for news from their president (lines 11–17). **5.** Sample answer: They stood for the national anthem out of respect and to show solidarity with the nation; they stayed standing in silence to gather themselves after hearing the address; and they hugged each other to give and take comfort (lines 33–41). **6.** Sample answer: The radio served as the family hearth, a place around which they would gather. It also offered warmth through FDR's reassuring voice and tone (lines 11–41).

Informational Text Passages

Passage 9: Squishy Foam

1. C; Sample answer: I think that *controlled* means that the recipe is designed to be safe even though there are chemicals involved. **2.** Sample answer: Step 3 says to mix the liquid glue with 1½ cups of water. So, water is the material used to dilute the glue (lines 17–19). **3.** Sample answer: You must follow the directions in the order given, but you can collect materials and tools in any order, as long as you assemble them all. Also, numbers that precede measurement amounts could be confusing or misread. **4.** Sample answers: pancake syrup, glue, oil, honey, and dish liquid. **5.** Sample answer: The sentence in parentheses is not part of the directions, but explains the chemical reaction that takes place in that step (lines 22–25). **6.** Sample answer: This is a science recipe about chemical reactions. Maybe the ingredients would react differently if they were mixed in metal or plastic bowls with metal or plastic spoons.

Passage 10: Please Re-Boot

1. D; Sample answer: At first I thought of the other *compliment* until I realized that that meaning didn't make sense. Thinking about outfits whose parts belong together, the writer mentioned her raincoat. **2.** Sample answer: The insoles don't stay in place, which makes the boots uncomfortable to wear (lines 15–18). **3.** Sample answer: She presents an unexpected problem, followed by a request for a logical solution. She begins with the facts of her purchase, explains the problem and her attempted solutions, and then asks for a refund based on the company's stated policy. **4.** Sample answer: It begins with the name and address of a business; it has a formal salutation that ends with a colon; it ends with a polite closing and the writer's full name and address. A friendly letter would be more casual and informal, perhaps less orderly (lines 1–6, 28–32). **5.** Sample answer: Apart from describing these two facts of her story, it also shows that Raven is a reasonable person who first tried to solve the problem in her own way (lines 19–24). **6.** Sample answer: Yes. The letter maintains a polite, proper, and calm tone throughout; it clearly states Raven's problem in a detailed and well-organized narrative; it is never angry or insulting, but offers a reasonable solution in line with the company's rules and promises.

Passage 11: Considering Competition

1. A; Sample answer: *Disparate* reminded me of the word *separate*, so I thought it could mean "not the same," or "distinctive." An opposite of that would be *comparable*. **2.** Sample answer: The writer wonders whether the amount and intensity of competition in American culture is becoming a problem (lines 1–5, 12–15, 18–21, 24–27, 33–39). **3.** Sample answer: I think the writer poses questions to stimulate readers to react to and question the ideas presented. Or the author may also be seeking answers to these questions. **4.** Sample answer: No. I think that the author accepts and respects some healthy competition. The writer even includes the phrase "a healthy dose of competitiveness" (lines 1–4, 16–21, 33–35). **5.** Answers will vary. Accept reasonable responses that students can justify. **6.** Answers will vary. Accept reasonable, complete responses that answer the question and provide supporting details.

Passage 12: Backstage at Theater Camp

1. C; Sample answer: *Tangible* means something actual or real that you can touch, do, or see. Passion is an internal feeling, not a skill to learn and show. **2.** Sample answer: She was hoping for a broad range of classes and coaching sessions to prepare her for her future goal to be a famous stage performer (lines 14–23). **3.** Sample answer: Divas are attention-craving performers who are full of themselves, which can make them difficult to work with. Iris recognizes their talent, but dislikes their self-absorption (lines 24–26). **4.** Sample answer: The tone is conversational, familiar, and humorous. Iris uses exaggeration, wit, and unexpected spelling to make her points about her dissatisfaction with camp. **5.** Sample answer: I think she wants to grab Jamie's attention with the dramatic complaints about the food, build sympathy for her plight, and prepare Jamie for complaints about the camp program. **6.** Sample answer: It tells me that Iris trusts Jamie; that Jamie is a close friend who knows Iris's family, has a sense of humor, high standards, and knows about theater and performing.

Passage 13: Tablet, Scroll, Text

1. C; Sample answer: I knew that A was a different meaning of *uniform* and D was irrelevant. So, I picked C as a better synonym than B. **2.** Sample answer: The writer has selected the words of an expert in the field of language history, which lends credibility to the arguments that follow. It also engages readers by making them ponder the meaning of that quotation (lines 1–7). **3.** Sample answer: Ancient cave art was a form of written communication that used pictures rather than words (lines 17–19). **4.** Sample answer: *Globalization* has the root word *globe*. The suffixes *-al* and *-ize* mean "to make" (to make like a globe) and *-tion* signals a noun form. So *globalization* is a noun for the idea that the whole world is interconnected. **5.** Sample answer: Both show tablets from different time periods; the first is an ancient carved stone tablet; the second is a 21st-century electronic device commonly known as a tablet. Both present written language (lines 23–25). **6.** Sample answer: The need for people of all languages and cultures to communicate makes it logical to limit the number of written languages used. Globalization calls for more standardized written languages for ease of communication.

Passage 14: *Lincoln*: A Movie Review

1. C; Sample answer: I reread the paragraph with *kudos* in it and saw that the reviewer was complimenting the film crews, so I picked C—a great achievement (lines 21–28). **2.** Sample answer: The tone is familiar, casual, witty, and somewhat sarcastic. The reviewer uses expressions like "no such luck" and "What a snoozer" to express disappointment (lines 7, 13, 14–20). **3.** Sample answer: Knowing that a movie set during the Civil War wouldn't have car chases, the reviewer uses this absurd description to highlight the lack of action in the film (lines 8–13). **4.** Sample answer: To persuade readers that the review is valid, it offers opinions supported by details and examples, but also acknowledges some of the film's strong points. **5.** Sample answer: It is a side comment, as though the reviewer is reminding readers of his or her qualifications and knowledge. **6.** Sample answer: The writer tries to be clever and funny, and to show that he is insightful and takes movies seriously. But he sounds arrogant, dismissive, and too casual, even ignorant, about some of the historical details he criticizes (lines 12–31).

Passage 15: Turning Point

1. C; Sample answer: I inferred from my reading of the passage that choices A and B are too literal to make sense. So, I picked C, interpreting sisters as female partners in a struggle. **2.** Sample answer: They had grown tired of so many years of waiting to get the vote that they felt the need to attempt new tactics (lines 1–6). **3.** Sample answer: Sentiment had been building for years, and finally reached the *tipping point*—a turning point, when something had to happen, and the long-sought goal became a reality (lines 28–34). **4.** Sample answer: Like soldiers on guard, they stood watch quietly. It was not a loud protest, but constant. They supported and guarded an ideal. Maybe they chose to be silent because it symbolized that they had no voice without the vote (lines 5–9, 28–34). **5.** Sample answer: "Notorious prison" and "abusive, inhumane treatment" (lines 10–12) help build sympathy for the imprisoned women. "Courage and sacrifices of the countless women..." (line 32) highlights that the struggle for women's suffrage was long and arduous, and involved many participants. **6.** Sample answer: The provocative poster puts all women in one large, negative category with convicts and lunatics. Its power comes from making no distinction between women and criminals or the insane.

Passage 16: Who Influences Young People?

1. C; Sample answer: Of the given choices, the kind of people I think would make best use of the ideas discussed are probably school guidance counselors. **2.** Sample answer: The speaker believes that the people who can most strongly influence the opinions of the young are creative artists (lines 24–41). **3.** Sample answer: It means to notice and respond to a message, idea, concept, value, etc., and eventually to take it to heart and make it your own (lines 24–36). **4.** Sample answer: A potent image moves you with its force, emotion, surprise, or unique message. The effect can be immediate or can build over time (lines 24–41). **5.** Sample answer: I think it is effective to begin the speech by summarizing and then refuting the viewpoints expressed by previous speakers. This organizational plan paves the way for this speaker's point of view (lines 5–23). **6.** Answers will vary. Sample answers: I disagree with Ai Weiwei. In my opinion, the world isn't really changing all that much. And I don't believe that artists care about change or influence as much as about beauty, self-expression, creativity, and acknowledgement. Or: I agree. The world is always changing and artists will create work that they hope will have an impact on the ways things change.

Passage 17: Perk-Up!

1. C; Sample answer: By reading the nutrition label, I saw that 1 serving of Perk-Up provides 100% of a person's daily need for vitamin C. **2.** Sample answer: No. The introductory sentence states that it is available "in select areas." **3.** Sample answer: Using the nutrition label, I saw that 1 serving is 8 ounces, and that the container provides 4 servings. So 4 x 8 = 32 ounces, or 1 quart. **4.** Sample answer: It tops the list, which makes me think that there is more water in Perk-Up than any other ingredient. **5.** Sample answer: Perk-Up is supposed to be a soft drink that boosts energy and health. So, showing an athletic and fit person in mid-workout supports that claim. **6.** Make sure students have at least four reasonable questions. Sample questions: 1. Do all other energy drinks really taste that bad? 2. Who are all these satisfied Americans, and how many thousands are there? 3. What kind of trainers and health-care professionals were consulted? 4. Compared with what other things or drinks does Perk-Up "work best"? 5. Is containing 20% juice something to boast about?

Passage 18: GMO: Yes or No?

1. B; Sample answer: I substituted each phrase for *skeptical* to hear how it worked. Since skeptical people mistrust frankenfoods, I thought B was the best answer. **2.** Sample answer: The goal is to grab the reader's attention. It does it with an opening question that uses a provocative term, then provides information about a renowned monster of literary and film fame (lines 1–6). **3.** Sample answer: The roughly patched-together pear reminds us of the Frankenstein monster. It looks like a pear, but it has been altered dramatically. **4.** Sample answer: They worry that changes of the type done now can result in unanticipated changes down the road that could have terrible consequences (lines 36–40). **5.** Sample answer: The

closing paragraph doesn't restate or summarize the argument, as is often done. Rather, it simply poses three questions directly to readers, I think, to get them to keep thinking about the topic. **6.** Sample answer: The writer presents adequate information to allow readers to form their own opinions on this topic without guiding them in one direction or the other.

Passage 19: Letter of Application

1. C; Sample answer: I can tell by the table and the sentence in line 27 that a peer is a classmate of the writer. **2.** Sample answer: Due to a lifelong interest in mathematics, Eleni seeks to attend a high school where math gets top priority (lines 6–16). **3.** Sample answer: She wants to show the admission team that she's a well-rounded person despite her major interest in statistics and that she would likely contribute to the school in many ways (lines 30–34). **4.** Sample answer: It may be unusual to do this, but it makes sense for Eleni to have included something statistical. Still, I'm not sure it belongs in this kind of letter. **5.** Sample answer: The paragraph about science seems weak in contrast to the strong math section that precedes it. She should have added more details about her science interest instead of bragging about her high test scores (lines 17–20). **6.** Sample answer: Eleni is a strong, confident student whose many interests complement her love of mathematics. She is well-rounded, sociable, and active, and seems to have clear plans for the future.

Passage 20: Fine Art vs. Folk Art

1. D; Sample answer: I read each pair of words in context to test whether they have similar meanings. It wasn't until choice D that the two words seemed nearly interchangeable. **2.** Sample answer: Fine art is considered legitimate because it is approved by museums, art schools, and other renowned institutions. But folk art is "outsider" art, usually made by creative people who are not classically trained (lines 13–24). **3.** Sample answer: The writer contends that artists of any kind express a creative, inventive vision through their chosen medium (lines 25–28). **4.** Sample answer: A curator is in charge of a museum, its collection, and how to put together works into organized exhibits. **5.** Answers will vary. Sample answer: I think Tolson is saying that an artist first needs an idea, and only then can he or she apply the necessary techniques to bring that idea to life. **6.** Answers will vary. Accept reasonable explanations. Sample answer: I see the carved bench as only folk art because it blends a practical skill and function with a whimsical vision.

Passage 21: Proposition 43

1. A; Sample answer: The "Good Business?" paragraph mentions all but choice A as reasons to build the new stadium (lines 19–34). **2.** Sample answer: The "we" is either a particular editor writing on behalf of the publication, or an editorial team that together writes it. **3.** Answers will vary widely. Accept any reasonable response that uses text references and explains them. **4.** Sample answer: I know that the word *prohibit* means to ban or prevent. A *prohibitive* cost must be so expensive that opponents want to prevent it from happening. **5.** Sample answer: Acting in self-interest means doing something to benefit yourself above others. The writer believes that supporters of the stadium stand to benefit from it far more than the community would (lines 19–34, 42–76). **6.** Sample answer: The closing paragraph summarizes the writer's conclusion that it would be far better for the community if voters reject Proposition 43.

Passage 22: Launch, Circuit, Land

1. B; Sample answer: I read all the choices, and B is the best. In lines 15–16, the text says "any pilot who hopes to fly solo must undertake formal instruction…", so I assume this is done to earn a certificate, like a license, that proves you're ready. **2.** Sample answer: The history of aviation has an abundance of famous pioneers whose… **3.** Sample answer: It's a nice touch to use a flying metaphor in a piece about flight. On another level, spreading your wings means to leave your comfort zone and try something new, like a baby bird as it first leaves its nest. **4.** Sample answer: The Lavenders support their son in pursuing his interests. Though they may fear for him, they encourage him and help him further his opportunities (lines 10–17, 30–36). **5.** Sample answer: The fuselage is the main body of an aircraft; the pilot sits inside it. The fuselage of a glider must be lightweight because the glider lacks its own source of power and can coast longer if it weighs less. **6.** Answers will vary. Sample answer: Callum is a fast learner, calm, able to plan ahead and control his emotions, and seems adventurous but not reckless. He might pursue a career in aviation, exploration, adventure, engineering, or science. He might become a glider instructor.

Passage 23: Miracle on Ice

1. D; Sample answer: The previous sentence tells that Coach Brooks had "tried to elevate his players' confidence." So, I think choice D most closely means that (lines 18–20). **2.** Sample answer: The United States and the Soviet Union were long-time Cold War antagonists; since the countries were rivals, so were their teams (lines 8–10). **3.** Sample answer: To me, this is an effective beginning. The writer opens with an emotional quotation from a sportscaster who was there, which immediately grabs readers' interest. Then come statistics and colorful language to set the scene and stir interest even more. I couldn't wait to learn about this game that I never even heard of (lines 1–7). **4.** Sample answer: It shows that people admire Herb Brooks enough to make a statue of him. **5.** Sample answer: The writer compares the U.S. victory over the Soviets in the hockey game to a high school football team beating Super Bowl champs—a highly unlikely, nearly unimaginable outcome (lines 24–27). **6.** Sample answer: Not really. That the American team beat the Soviets must have seemed like a miracle, like a case of divine intervention. But the victory was hard-fought and really happened. A more literal term might be "an upset." The widely embraced nickname "Miracle on Ice" stuck because it was dramatic and recalls the profound pride, joy, and sense of unity.

Passage 24: El Sistema

1. B; Sample answer: A and D were specifically mentioned in lines 29–31; C makes sense in light of the program's goals, so I picked B. **2.** Sample answer: Because Dudamel is internationally famous, using his name and telling people that he went through the El Sistema program lends credibility (lines 3–7). **3.** Sample answer: In this usage, to *inform* means "to be the characteristic quality of" or "be the essence of." So the writer is saying that no matter how hard participants work, joy and purpose are always there. **4.** Sample answer: I imagine a joyful, busy, and active place where participants are fully engaged, supportive of one another, respectful, and enthusiastic about being part of this experience. **5.** Sample answer: I think the writer means that the most important goal is to guide children to feel safe, accept personal and group responsibility, develop confidence, and become lifelong achievers rather than just to train musicians for orchestras (lines 7–20, 32–37). **6.** Sample answer: "To play" literally means to make music on an instrument, but can also mean being a member of a group, exploring joyfully and with a sense of curiosity, or formulating strategies for one's life. "To fight" sounds combative, but for El Sistema it means to fight one's insecurities or outside problems by finding a hopeful purpose through music.

Passage 25: Eccentric Family Staycation

1. B; Sample answer: This essay is about a member of the team that worked on the Mars Rover project. We know that the Mars Rover landed on that planet to send back pictures and data, so I think B is the most logical answer. **2.** Sample answer: Dr. Oh, the father, had to shift time for his work. His family decided to do it, too, for a better sense of the challenges facing scientific researchers (lines 21–22). **3.** Sample answer: The word *neologists* appears in the paragraph about how the family made up new words. I know that the prefix *neo-* means "new," the Greek root *log* means "word," and the suffix *-ist* means "one who practices." So *neologists* must be people who make up new words (lines 17–20). **4.** Sample answer: The Ohs seem to be a close-knit family, adventurous, curious, fun-loving, and eager to experience new things. **5.** Sample answer: Circadian rhythms describe the body's natural biological patterns that last about 24 hours. The Oh family figured out how to adjust their circadian rhythms to coordinate with Mars time. The phrase is "adjust their body clocks" (lines 5–16, 25–26). **6.** Sample answer: The orbital paths of planets around the sun are elliptical, so the distance between any planet and the sun changes as the planet travels. Therefore, using a mean distance is one consistent way to make a comparison.

25 Complex Text Passages to Meet the Common Core: Literature and Informational Texts, Grades 7–8 © 2014 by Scholastic Teaching Resources